The Sacred Halls of St. Disaster

(A Year

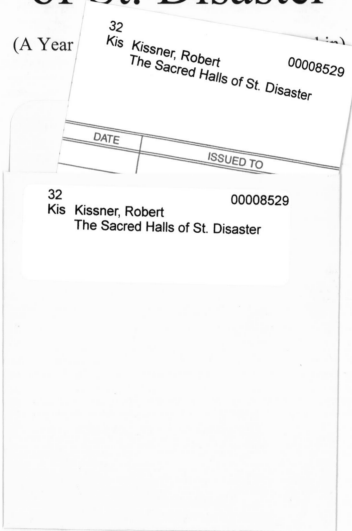

For Idgit Randall and Willoughby Anne:
may your gifts elevate you to heights I could never imagine.

Foreword

This book began as a doodle, an absent-minded sketch that quickly evolved into an obsession, a number-two Ticonderoga blueprint of a building I had not seen in thirty years. As a first grader I had no reference point, so to my point of view, everything about the place was normal, common. It was not until after the fire trucks came and went and I began attending public school that I began to realize I had experienced a living relic. Unfortunately, that realization came in small increments over a span of several years, and by the time I made my first efforts to reconstruct the experience in my mind, the building was gone.

Images and historical documentation have been scarce, even in this digital age. In their stead I began to have dreams—some real, some surreal—seen through the eyes of a towheaded boy out of my distant past. I relived the smell of over-waxed hardwood and old carpet, the hollow footfalls in enclosed stairwells, and the chilling sight of smoke and flames erupting from the roof of the only school I had ever known. Years later a classmate would sing, "Mine eyes have seen the glory of the burning of the school." It remains a common fantasy among school-age children, but all I could think, then and now, is *You don't know, man. You just don't know.*

So I wrote the first paragraph, hoping to jog a memory of how my homeroom linked to, say, the cafeteria. Something about that first page made me laugh, so I wrote a second page. I realized very quickly that while I had begun this project in effort to yank up the entire building out of my swampy subconscious, the story of a confused six-year-old was starting to emerge instead.

I wanted to continue exploring those sacred halls, but I was fascinated with the memories, lessons, and even some tall tales caught in orbit around this young boy. Many of his experiences are my own, but like Twain's Tom Sawyer, Timothy Larkin became the hybrid of a handful of youngsters out of my past. To quote Chris McCord, the finest principal I have ever met, "I took Ritalin before taking Ritalin was cool." What social skills I learned, I learned by trial and error, and the errors seemed amplified in first and second grade. My struggles with Attention Deficit Hyperactive Disorder necessarily became a part of Timothy's wanderings, as did my peers and teachers' reactions to my failures and triumphs.

My primary hope is that this book will make you laugh, but I will not feel successful if that is your only reaction. I included a fair amount of earthy humor because that is precisely what stands out in the memory banks of most kids, and it will usually be the first thing to come across when a boy sits down to tell you about his day. I also included what I hope will be valuable insights into the thoughts and motivations of a child whose behavior requires medicine to temper. I am not a counselor, nor am I a psychiatrist, and this is not an attempt to create a definitive work on the subject. Apart from a few episodes in the life of Timothy Larkin, however, perhaps this is a rambling homily designed to help you appreciate with a more open heart that person in your life who so often drives you to distraction. May that appreciation grow into a love you never realized could go any deeper.

I also hope to honor Dr. Pascal Spino for his peerless work as my pediatrician, my parents for their battle-tested patience and love, and my beautiful children and their remarkable mother.

Finally, I wish to recognize Pittsburgh's Sisters of Mercy, who taught me for two years. To use today's vernacular, in many ways they were *old school*, but when it came to reigning in the likes of a Timothy Larkin or Bobby Kissner, I believe they knew what they were doing.

St. Xavier's Academy, located along the Lincoln Highway in Unity Township between Greensburg and Latrobe, Pennsylvania, was destroyed by fire on Thursday, March 16, 1972. I was there when it happened. I began to write a book about the building, but that book turned into something else entirely.

A few months ago while noodling around on the Internet, I stumbled across a couple old pictures of the place. Know what? It looked even finer than I remembered.

Robert M. Kissner
The Woodlands, Texas

St. Géneviève of the Oaks

I attended first and second grade at St. Géneviève's Academy, which is appropriate, because many people recognize St. Géneviève as the patron saint of disasters. It's been said that inanimate objects have learned to recognize the sound of my approaching footsteps, and some have developed the means of retreating from my path. I can't be certain, but I think I've seen the mirror on the medicine chest flinch when I've stepped into the bathroom. Most of these jittery objects belong in my house, where they've been able to meet and compare notes. But poor St. Géneviève's, positioned as she was along a winding country lane in the middle of nowhere, didn't hear me coming. She soon figured things out, though. You might not believe it, but I'm pretty sure that building was alive.

St. Géneviève's Academy sat on the south edge of an old oak grove a few hundred yards off the road leading out of town. Three stories tall, her stone face bearded by a century's growth of ivy, she glowered through arched windows across an emerald lawn bordered by massive oaks and crosshatched by moss-covered walkways. In winter the leafless trees looked like huge vulture talons flexed against the sky, as if somebody tried to bury a flock of buzzards but didn't dig the holes quite deep enough.

The main section of the school was L-shaped, with wings stretching north and east. A grey wooden porch ran the lengths of these two wings. During recess the porch became a marvelous pair of aircraft carriers for imaginary fighter planes—Corsairs in corduroys—taking to the skies for fifteen-minute missions after lunch. With arms outstretched in tight formation, my friend Clark and I swooped in low over the girls playing hopscotch and strafed them without mercy. The girls

1

retaliated with anti-aircraft volleys of a fiery verbal nature: *You're so immature!*

The yellowed halls at St. Génevière's breathed and watched me as we marched single file along her corridors to some remote corner of the building. The first grade classroom sat on the second floor at the far end of the north wing. The ceiling in that room towered above us as tall, multi-paned windows overlooked the western lawn. Afternoons in May were often so muggy the ceiling seemed to disappear in the clouds. On October mornings you could imagine fog creeping between the desks. From our corner classroom any destination seemed miles away. A far stretch up the hall, the girls' bathroom sat at the intersection of the north and east wings. (The boys' room, with its dim light and bad smells, occupied an out-of-the-way space in a dark corner one-and-a-half stories below.) This intersection also served as a landing for the Grand Staircase, which fed the east wing first floor with its long cascade of red granite steps and brass handrail down the center.

The east wing began as a balcony overlooking the Grand Staircase. It broadened along the way to form a landing for the Green Staircase, a narrower flight of steps reaching over the Grand to the third floor. Beyond this landing along the east wing sat the kindergarten room, which was wide enough to have windows facing both north and south. There were impossible ceilings in this room as well, supported by four fat columns rising skyward out of the floor. At Christmastime Sister Beryl wrapped these columns in delicate red streamer, giving them the appearance of gargantuan peppermint sticks. Her students knew better than to touch them, for they knew her wrath. I didn't, however, having attended kindergarten elsewhere. But I soon would.

The kindergarten room had Dutch doors, sliced horizontally across the middle. (It crossed my mind once to cut my bedroom door in half the same way, but I couldn't get the cord on my dad's saber saw to reach. Probably a good thing.) Sister Beryl always kept their bottom halves closed so none of her flock would escape, but she kept the top halves open year round. One spring morning, a disoriented thrush flew through one of Sister Beryl's doors and out the other. Even the most veteran teacher might've struggled to regain control of her class after such an invasion, but Sister Beryl, with her beefy arms and overhanging brow, silenced any potential shenanigans with a single, preemptive *SsssT!*

Beyond the kindergarten room sat the second floor landing of the Gold Staircase. Narrower than the Grand, but more fun to descend because of its treacherous switchbacks between floors, the Gold Staircase serviced all three stories. A shoulder-high strip along the pale gold walls had been worn grey by legions of ornery boys jostling with each other on their way down. Here, a monstrous iron bell roosted on a tall wishbone stand, a frayed cotton rope hanging from its arm.

The bell could've been a little brother to that famous one frozen on display in Philadelphia. As if by some sinister spell, liquid darkness obscured the bell's innards, including the clapper. If the thing ever rang, it would likely summon gargoyles out of the rafters to storm down on us. Daring pranksters tempted to tug on the rope were reminded of the consequences—one sharp rap to the knuckles upon returning to the classroom.

Upperclassmen, who wore real neckties (as opposed to our elementary clip-on kind), pondered in the chalk-dusty chambers beyond the kindergarten room, while immediately below lurked Sister Gwendolyn, the principal at St. Géneviève's. I had heard about her office, but not from anyone who'd ever seen it, mind you. Those folks were all dead—out buried with the vultures. Her office was sealed with a thick lead door. The knob was a steel wagon wheel that was always cold to the touch. The walls were lined with sharp hooks where she hung fat slabs of raw meat. Instead of a desk, she pulled her bear-clawed chair up to a black boulder that had fallen from space. Flowers wilted the moment they entered the room. She liked that. The floor was carpeted with shredded tin cans that hid a trapdoor—the secret passage to the oblong pine box where she slept. Her telephone bled when she dialed it.

At least, that's what I'd heard.

If the north and east wings formed an L, the east and south wings made a T. Anyone swooping down the Gold Staircase at terminal velocity would spill straight out the main doors (or against them if they were locked) and onto the front lawn. If he managed instead to grab the newel post at the foot of the stairs and whip hard about to the left, he'd find himself facing the mysterious south wing. Nobody ever ran more than two steps into the south wing without hitting the brakes, for students entered the south wing only on very special occasions.

The south wing began as a narrow corridor in the shadow of the Gold Staircase. A rickety brown door on the right led to an odd, sloping hall leading to my favorite room at St. Géneviève's, the library. Planted half-a-story into the ground, the library jutted out from the corner formed by the east and south wings like a wart between your toes. Small windows between bookshelves offered a bug's eye view of a weedy courtyard where people didn't go. But glory, there were books! We could find out about planets or dinosaurs or even fighter planes. Upperclassmen went there too, to find out about whatever they need to find out about. Their books were always bigger than ours, but ours always had better pictures. No matter how old and smart I get, I think I'll always appreciate a good picture. Granddad Larkin says, "A picture tells a thousand words, but a picture window kills a thousand birds." He's a wise man.

Speaking of windows, along the south wing beyond the library were windows to the right, looking onto the weedy courtyard and the library in its little pit. To the left was the first of two very large, very fancy rooms. Sister Barbara, my homeroom teacher for first and second grade, called the first room the Lounge. Every morning at ten, the older sisters met there on the red and blue couches for tea. The room just beyond, decorated in purples and greens, was called the Parlor. Nobody met there; that room was just too fancy to be any fun.

Directly across the hall from the Parlor were the heavy oak double doors to the Chapel. When opened, the door hinges creaked like a galleon's masts bending in a gale. A stone aisle separated the many rows of pews to the left and right, then split to form a cross in the floor just before the altar. The Chapel dozed in dim candle light even during Mass, making it impossible to make out the fine details in the high vaulted ceiling, which might as well have been hung above the clouds in the midnight air. Sister Barbara brought us to the Chapel one morning to show us a tall beeswax candle. I'd never seen anything like it—sort of like a baseball bat made of lace and glue. It would have been a shame to burn it, I thought. The Chapel impressed me, not only because of its immensity, but also because it was the only place where I had ever heard Sister Barbara whisper.

The Convent lay farther along the south wing, occupying all three floors. The younger sisters, the ones who weren't afraid of high places, lived in rooms on the third floor. The very old sisters, who could no longer get out of bed by themselves, lived on the first floor. On Halloween we dressed in our costumes and paraded by the old women in their beds. They all loved Annie, who had dressed like a princess, and they all wanted to pet Felicia, who looked like a cat. Clark, who had dressed as a clown, made all of them laugh. I was a skeleton that year, with glittery glow-in-the-dark bones and a green crack down the center of my skull mask. I don't think they liked my costume as much. Maybe it made them think of vultures.

St. Génevieve's was all of this: the building with its shadows and corners and points, the books and windows, nuns in veils, and the Convent—where prayers were whispered and where disaster would strike.

Sister Barbara

When I die and my soul takes off for Heaven, I want my body to go *Pfffffffffffffffffffffffffffff* all around the room like a runaway balloon. Then the doctor can pick up my body, all flat and floppy and a whole lot smaller, examine it for a moment, announce to the world "He's dead," and tuck it into his shirt pocket.

I started thinking about that after Sister Barbara taught us about Heaven and bodies and souls. Even though my family makes it to church every week, where there's plenty of talk about those kinds of things, Sister Barbara did an especially good job explaining it all. And she did it in a way I never would have heard in church. She said she could take me out back, take me apart the way a monkey peels a banana, spread all my parts across a sheet, and never find my soul. Oh, you might hear a statement like that in church, but you'd never hear what happened next.

Clark burped.

It wasn't loud, but it was wet and greasy, like an airborne bathroom sponge. Right away the air went a little yellow. People don't do things like that in church.

Clark looked at Sister Barbara like he'd just said a dirty word, and she looked right back at him like she was thinking maybe she should've taken *him* apart instead. People don't do things like that in front of Sister Barbara, either. But then she said, "It's like that burp we just heard from Mr. Bernard over there. Mr. Bernard had been carrying that burp around with him all afternoon, but when it was time for the burp to leave his body, it simply left. It's gone."

I couldn't believe it. Sister Barbara was talking about that burp as if she'd planned it. "You won't find a trace of it

7

anywhere in his body; however," she continued, "judging by the way Mr. Larkin is breathing through his shirt sleeve, you can tell that the burp still has a life of its own!"

She didn't know the half of it. That burp smelled like someone had clocked me with a rancid muskrat. Once when I was hunting salamanders in a creek near home, I found an old pop bottle buried in the mud along the bank. The label was gone, and the drink had been replaced with dark green ooze. I tipped the bottle to see what would come out, and boy was I sorry I did! Mixed into the ooze was a brown blob about the size of a mouse. The ooze was cold and stringy and mustardy, the raunchiest thing I'd ever smelled—up to the point when Clark burped anyway. Clark liked to catch a burp in his cheeks and hold it there to ferment for a second, and then he'd tele-graph it into the face of anyone unfortunate enough to be sit-ting nearby. It always made me mad when he did it because it always reeked, and because I was never any good at doing it myself.

But I understood what Sister Barbara was trying to say. Even though Clark had paid close attention while eating what-ever unholy thing he'd discovered in his lunchbox, once lunch was over, he'd shifted his attention to something else. By the time the burp came along a couple hours later and polluted the air, lunch had been forgotten. All our attention was now fo-cused on the burp (and how to get away from it). In the same way, we worry about our bodies for a while, but when the soul jumps out, that's the thing we should be most concerned about.

Sister Barbara was my homeroom teacher. She also taught Reading. She was my favorite teacher at St. Géneviève's. Even though she yelled at me a lot, I usually de-served it. It was like getting yelled at by your grandmother. When Grandma yells at you, you've been *bad*. Sister Barbara had been irritated with Clark for burping, but she felt it was more important at the moment to keep talking about our souls. So instead of yelling at Clark or making him stand in the corner until she was done, she found a way to use the burp in her lesson. Of course, I can't say whether or not she would have been able to continue if she'd actually smelled it.

Sister Barbara, who was named for the patron saint of artillery, was about as tall as my mom, who is taller than I am, but shorter than a lot of people. She was older than Mom and Dad, but younger than my grandparents. I never saw what color hair she had because she always wore a habit, that black or grey dress and veil that the nuns at St. Génevieve's wore. No one knew if her hair was long or short or brown or blond or grey, if it was parted down the middle or down the side. Sometimes I wondered if she even bothered combing it in the morning or if she just wadded it up in a ball and stuck it into her veil. I never had the guts to ask her about it though. If I were a nun and had to wear a veil, I don't think I'd ever comb my hair.

She wore little round glasses and she had strong hands. Every now and then when the class was lined up to walk someplace, I'd make a bad decision and have to hold her hand. My dad has a tool in his woodshop called a vise. It's made of two black blocks of iron and a crank handle. He uses it when he wants to squish two things together and keep them that way. My dad's vise could have learned a thing or two from Sister Barbara about squishing things.

Dad said Sister Barbara was a no-nonsense kind of person. Most of the time she was very serious, but I think she had to be when Clark and I were around. There were times when she'd smile and it was almost as good as a hug. We knew we had to get to work in her class, though. She never had to tell anyone more than once to get busy. Even I knew better. There were times when she would glare at me from over her glasses, and it would straighten me out faster than one of those little pills I have to take every morning.

Speaking of those pills, Sister Barbara knew I had to take them, and she could always tell when I'd missed a dose. "Mr. Larkin," she would say as I drummed on my desk or made wise cracks in a squeaky baby voice or made inappropriate (but really, really funny) comments about Nina Campbell, "did somebody forget to take his pill this morning?" The truth is, I never actually *forgot* to take my pill. My mom made sure it was on my placemat every morning when I sat down for breakfast. She'd stuff it inside a gumdrop so it wouldn't taste so bad when I crunched it. But sometimes I'd stick it in my pocket, or worse. We have a ficus tree in a huge planter in the living room. It's tall and leafy, and for a while it was pretty well behaved because it took one or two of those little pills each week, right into the mulch. I got caught when Dad spotted a parade of ants marching along the living room wall and into the planter, obviously attracted to the gumdrops. Then we had a long talk about how I take my pills so I can stay *on task*, which is Latin for *on track*, which is English for not fidgeting or making goofy noises or acting like an idiot.

One Sunday when the children's choir performed at my church, Sister Barbara came to hear us. It came as quite a shock to realize she did stuff on weekends. When I saw her, I waved right in the middle of the song. I don't even think I finished the song; I just stood there waving. After the service, my mom asked me if I would like for Sister Barbara to visit us for lunch. These days I'd be horrified at the thought of one of my teachers coming over to the house for anything, even if it was to tell me I'd won a hundred dollars. I would've figured I'd have to do a whole bunch of math first. But in first grade, having Sister Barbara come over was the greatest thing in the world. We had roast beef and baked potatoes. I did my best to sit up straight and use all my manners. Everything went well, except for when Charlie, my stupid little brother, leaned to one side and squeaked a greaser right at the table. I personally outgrew that kind of thing when Sister Barbara came over.

After lunch we had pie in the living room. Mom and Dad and Sister Barbara had coffee and talked about what goes on in little boys' minds. It was a grown-up conversation, and I got restless. Before I ran off to play with Charlie, I heard Sister Barbara make a comment about what an admirable tree that ficus was—high praise from Sister Barbara. Admirable, she said. I decided at that point not to hide any more of my pills.

Sister Helga's Class and the
Glass Animal Boxes

Monday and Thursday mornings we had music class in the Dungeon. Most people think of dungeons as being cold, musty places with cobwebs, torture devices caked with dried blood, and wet stone walls. That doesn't really describe the room where we had music. Its walls weren't stone.

Sister Barbara would line us up in single file, boy-girl-boy-girl, and lead us deep into the bowels of St. Géneviève's. Down the Grand Staircase, a U-turn to the left on the first floor landing, down a half-staircase that could have been the Grand's little brother, and then past the auditorium, which would have been a great place to have music class. It had a stage and a grand piano and everything. Instead, the auditorium, with its parquet floor and high ceiling, was where we had gym class when the weather turned.

The boys' restroom sat at the end of the hall beyond the auditorium. While the girls' room always appeared bright and sunny at the top of the Grand Staircase—or so it seemed each time Clark and I caught a peek through the swinging door—the boys' room squatted in the shadows directly below, crouched like a rabid bobcat, ready to pounce on anyone daring to enter while breathing through his nose. The odor would poke its foul yellow claws into my sinuses and twist them around until they found what they were rooting for. Then I'd walk around for most of the morning with traces of boys' room still stuck in my snot.

"Doc, I can't seem to be able to shake this horrible smell in my nose. . ."

"Well son, the preliminary lab report suggests you have a bad case of lavatorius mucotosis. *In layman's terms, Bathroom Boogers."*

Sister Barbara always halted the line on the way to music so we could all use the restroom, but she wanted us to be quick. No sit-downs, please.

Not that I would ever stay in there long enough for a sit-down. I once saw a movie about germs, and when the cameras moved in really close, the germs looked like ugly brown dragons with long beards and green tattoos. The downstairs boys' room seemed like just the place to have a brown dragon latch onto your bottom, and I never wanted to let that happen to me.

She told us to wait our turns, wash our hands without splashing, and then get back in line. One day she heard us all laughing when were supposed to be doing our business, and she walked *right into* the boys' room and caught David DeFloria and Richard Irwin peeing in the same urinal! They were trying to hit streams, but they told her they were just trying to be quick. I don't think she bought it because they still had to clap erasers during recess.

After we'd used the restroom, Sister Barbara would lead us down the Black Staircase. I liked the Black Staircase, even though it was uglier than the others. The floor tiles were chipped and coming up in places, and it always smelled like bologna. The great part was there were windows in the left wall that looked across the grass in the courtyard.

The courtyard didn't get much sun, so the weak light coming through those windows looked like the last breath of the sun before being swallowed by storm clouds.

Even though the steps went a long way down, the ceiling didn't. It stayed level, as if the floor didn't fall away at all. So did the courtyard windowsills. By the time the staircase landed in the basement, the ceiling was a long way up, and nobody was tall enough to look out the windows. A wall reached down from the ceiling above and met with the basement ceiling over the foot of the stairs. There were always dirty handprints on that wall where sixth graders had jumped off the bottom step and slapped it as they headed into the dining room. Clearly, they didn't have Sister Barbara walking with them.

Sister Barbara would lead us into the dining room where we could smell what the cafeteria ladies were cooking for lunch. There was always a warm, brown, meaty aroma emanating from the kitchen, but when a cafeteria lady at St. Géneviève's served green beans, she didn't use a spoon. She just stuck her hand right into the pan, nothing but a plastic bag lashed to her wrist with a rubber band. That always made me uneasy, maybe because Mom and Dad always yelled whenever I stuck my hands in my food.

The basement sat in another world, directly below the Chapel, but somehow miles deeper. The dining room ceiling was low, as if the weight of the Chapel pushed it down. Several square pillars held up the ceiling, and I could imagine them straining under the pressure like the arms of a circus strong man who'd forgotten to drink his milk. Our line snaked through the dining room and then to the left, along a broad corridor directly beneath the Chapel's main aisle.

You can't walk into a school anywhere in this country without seeing a glass display case. Most times they are built into the wall, but sometimes, like the ones at St. Géneviève's, such cases are independent pieces of furniture that stand freely and collect dust. Cases located near art rooms often feature paintings and small sculptures, and cases outside school gymnasiums are usually packed with trophies shaped like footballs and basketballs. Down this hall, just beyond the cafeteria, the glass display cases at St. Géneviève's were filled with dead animals. If an animal slithered, swam, crawled, or flew within a hundred miles of St. Géneviève's, it had a cousin stuffed and on display in one of those cases, and they stared at us with their beady glass eyes as we marched by.

One case had glass shelves lined with varnished salamanders and papery butterflies. Another contained a super-

15

structure of gnarled tree branches where a motley chorus of woodpeckers, finches, jays, and a crow assembled. At the very top a red-tailed hawk spread his wings to direct the choir. The big box at the end of the hall contained a bear, a bobcat, and a white-tailed deer. Then came the Dungeon.

An open portal at the end of the hall led to a dim passageway that zigzagged right, then left, past locked doors and rooms I never knew, and then right again, to the chamber of Sister Helga, who glared at us from beneath her veil while punishing her piano keys with her pink sausage fingers.

My mom had a music degree from a good college upstate, and both my parents sang in the church choir every Sunday. Mom taught piano to the kids in the neighborhood, and Dad knew every song on the radio. I was raised to believe music was a good thing, a gift to be unwrapped every time an instrument was touched or a note sung. Sister Helga seemed to believe music was a blue steel hatchet to be swung at little boys who misbehaved during her biweekly torture sessions. She never stood during class, but fired off every lecture from behind the piano. She looked very large in her nun's habit, and when she sat at the piano, yards of excess fabric cascaded over the bench like a black waterfall. So I never actually *saw* the piano bench. I just assumed it was there—*hoped* it was there—because the thought of her levitating behind the piano like a pink and black wrecking ball was too frightening to reckon with. In my two years at St. Géneviève's, I saw her walk just once. I was eating lunch in the dining room, my trusty Dr. Doolittle lunchbox in tow, when she came roaring up the hall. She looked like a thunderstorm rolling down from Canada, and all the dead animals hid their glass eyes in fright. She stirred up so much air when she trucked past the table that my napkin did a somersault in her slip stream.

Students in the Dungeon sat shoulder to shoulder in tight rows of hard folding chairs—uncomfortable, but perfect for the melding of choral voices or the sharing of flu germs. It was during Sister Helga's lecture on eighth notes that Clark

16

told me about his Aunt Meg, who spoke with a lisp. She didn't have a *lithp*, he told me, but a *lisshp*; and she sounded that way because she had too much *sshpit* between her *bicusshpidzh*. I knew what he was talking about. Back in kindergarten I had known a kid named Tommy Brewer, who must've had a lot of spit between his bicuspids, too. Nobody ever laughed at him, any more than anyone would laugh at someone for having eyebrows. In fact, we all sort of looked up to Tommy because we could recognize his voice, even when he whispered during naptime. He didn't care for it, though, because my kindergarten teacher, Mrs. Greypool, could recognize his voice too, and she always had something to say in response.

Now I would never make fun of Aunt Meg—Mom and Dad taught me not to be mean—but I really wanted to try out that wonderful *lisshp*. So when Sister Helga gave four-for-nothing (uh-*one-two-three-four*) and began to play, I began to sing:

> *Sshing a sshong of sshixh penssh, a pocket full of rye,*
> *Four and twenty blackbirdzzh baked in a pie . . .*

Somehow, Sister Helga heard me.

I've read that bats talk in high-pitched squeaks that people can't hear. They fly all over the place yelling at bugs—usually ugly things about the bugs' mothers. Bugs can't control their tempers, so when the bats yell at them, they yell back. That gets the bugs in trouble every time. They hover with their hands on their little bug hips, and about the time they think of something clever to say, the bats swoop in and eat them. I think Sister Helga could give a lecture on what she's heard the bats and bugs talking about.

"Timothy Nathaniel Larkin!" she bellowed, coming as close as I had ever seen to standing behind her piano. I think the piano may have flinched at her outburst; I know I did. "Stand up, young man!" For a boy of seven, being called a young man is rarely a sign of respect. I knew that, even then.

17

"Yes, Ma'am?" I answered, standing. My cousins had been raised to address their elders as Ma'am and Sir, and my brother Charlie and I had always snickered at their old-fashioned ways. But as I marveled at the six deep furrows in Sister Helga's flaming forehead and the way they made her bushy eyebrows flare like a crazed raven rocketing out of a blast furnace, I figured some old-fashioned manners were the key to my survival.

"Mr. Larkin," she proceeded, "are you aware that there are those who walk this earth with what is known as a speech impediment?" I had no idea what an impediment was, but it seemed appropriate to nod my head. "And Mr. Larkin, are you also aware that these afflicted people were born this way through no fault of their own?" I could hear my classmates chuckling all around me. I wondered if Valerie Dorazio, whom I secretly admired, was among those students laughing at my expense. *Surely not*, but I dared not look her way. "Let me ask you, Mr. Larkin," she continued, glaring at me from over her thick spectacles, "do you hear their derision? Do you feel their cold stares prying into the fibers of your shirt?"

I had to admit I could, and I began to see the point she was trying to make. The worst part was knowing that she would continue to make her point long after I understood. Again I nodded yes.

Speaking in a lower, less agitated register, Sister Helga said, "Now you have tasted a morsel of the humiliation these people feel each time they come in contact with ignorant young men such as yourself." She let that sink in, and then finished with the suggestion that I sit down and seek my entertainment through other, more conscientious avenues.

I shrugged at Clark, who shrugged back. He had no more idea than I did about seeking entertainment through more conscientious avenues. An avenue is a street, I reasoned. Conscientious means you're awake. At least that's what I assumed, because I could remember my dad telling me the story of a friend of his who fell while running at a swimming pool and was knocked un-conscientious. I couldn't understand what Sister Helga meant about waking up along an avenue, but I knew she was right about making fun of people. So when we sang the song again, I didn't lisp. Instead I substituted razzberries for all the S's. The split flew in delightful burts, and it seemed people were now laughing *with* me instead of *at* me.

I should have known better—I *did* know better—but at the moment I thought it was just a nicer way of singing the song than by making fun of people. Sister Helga didn't appreciate my logic. "Mr." she paused, closing her eyes and shaking her head for effect, "Larkin." The class fell silent, knowing they were about to take home a story they would share with their own children one day. "Find your place at the top of the page, and sing this song the way the composer intended for us to sing it."

Understand, I've always enjoyed being the center of attention if I've gone looking for it: there's something rewarding about stealing the show. The reward goes sour, however, when the star of the show hands over the microphone and steps off the stage in disgust. I squinted at the tadpole notes on the page, feeling like I had just gargled cat litter. I pretended not to know where we were. This time I did look toward Valerie Dorazio. For the first time I was aware of, I was the center of her attention.

"Miss Diorio," Sister Helga ordered, "please show Mr. Larkin where he is to begin." Cheryl Diorio (Rhymes with *the Oreo*) rose from her seat next to me and pointed to the word *Sing* with her spitty index finger. Then she returned to chewing on her nail. I had recently misplaced my wristwatch, but I could sense there was a lot of class time left. Besides, there were no period bells at St. Géneviève's, so Sister Helga could have kept the class until June, waiting to hear me sing the song. I began, hoping she would accompany me on the piano. She did not.

"Sing . . . a song . . . of six . . . pence, a . . . pocket full of rye . . ."

My breakfast began seething in my stomach like a caged leopard. It paced back and forth in its pit, clawing at the walls, devising its escape. Had there been another verse, the furious beast fuming behind my navel would have leaped for the freedom of the Dungeon's dusty floor. As it was, by the time I squeaked out the last part about the blackbird plucking off the maid's nose, I swallowed hard and managed to squelch the uprising in my gut.

"Terrible, Mr. Larkin," Sister Helga remarked as she shook her head again. "Absolutely—" and she paused, shaking her head some more and scanning the ceiling for the most devastating word, "terrible. Perhaps you would perform better for Sister Gwendolyn. You are dismissed, Mr. Larkin."

I was stunned. Sister Helga was sending me to Sister Gwendolyn. I was more afraid of Sister Gwendolyn than I was of Sister Helga. Sister Gwendolyn was not much taller than I was, nor was she as zeppelinesque as Sister Helga, but she had long fingers that she enjoyed pointing at people. Her eyes were sunken in deep shadows, lurking like hungry trapdoor spiders. When she shifted her gaze across a group of ne'er-do-wells, you could hear her eyeballs scrape against the back of her skull. To make it all worse, Sister Helga didn't bother to write a note for me to carry, which meant I'd be forced to explain my behavior to Sister Gwendolyn in my own words.

I set down my music book and weaved my way through a maze of knobby knees until I reached the aisle, then I gave one last pleading look to Sister Helga, hoping she would change her mind. She just maintained her unique version of the popular Impatient-With-Timothy look and tapped one bratwurst finger on the piano cabinet. Again I felt the stares of my classmates, probably even Valerie Dorazio. Oddly, the weight of their stares was heavier without their laughter, and my footfalls were deafening, even as I tiptoed out of the room.

20

The load fell away, though, as I closed the door behind me, and I set my mind to finding the words to explain to Sister Gwendolyn exactly why I'd dropped in for a visit during class time:

Hi, Sister Gwendolyn! My name is Clark Bernard . . .

Good morning, Sister Gwendolyn. I was sent by Sister Helga to see if you needed anything . . .

Sister Gwendolyn, have I ever told you how much you remind me of my mom?

I emerged from the zigzag corridor and faced the animals frozen in their glass mausoleum. The deer didn't seem to mind being so close to a bobcat and a bear. She just stood there, looking off at goodness-knows-what. In her sewn-up glory, she was probably trying to remember the last time she pooped. The red-tailed hawk looked angry, as if he had seen everything that had gone on in Sister Helga's class and wanted to give me some medicine. I had always liked the hawk, but at the moment I didn't have his sympathy.

My stomach rumbled to the warm meat loaf scent wafting up the hall from the cafeteria. Lunchtime was just around the corner, which meant my class would soon come snaking its way past the static menagerie. The smell from the kitchen carried with it a sudden truth that sliced through my terror like a foghorn through a soupy mist: after witnessing my foolishness firsthand, Sister Helga still trusted me to make my way to Sister Gwendolyn's office unescorted! Actually, she didn't trust my honesty so much as she trusted the long arm of fear she instilled in her students. Indeed, most students would have been pleased with the option to visit Sister Gwendolyn rather than facing the continuing bombardment of Sister Helga's wrath. While Sister Gwendolyn was certainly capable of wrath of her own, her anger would be second-hand, meaning she would not take my transgressions in Sister Helga's class personally. But Sister Helga failed when she overlooked my distractibility. It took only forty-five seconds and the comfortable scent of meat loaf to relieve me of my fears of Sister Gwendolyn.

I spotted a narrow gap between a pair of the glass boxes, the ones containing the reptiles and the birds. The space was no more than a foot wide, and I had a devil of a time scrunching in and getting comfortable. The cases were large—between five and eight feet long, five feet high, and two feet front-to-back. The sides and top were wood paneled, and the backs were mirrored. I was a snail, retreating farther and farther into my hiding spot, and I realized I had done well. I would be invisible to anyone prowling the hall: only those in active search mode would spot me in my dark shell of wood and glass. The class would come, I would slither from my spot and into line, and by the time I saw Sister Helga again, she would have found another target for her wrath.

The reptile case stood out from the wall a few inches—enough space for me to cram my leg—and I was able to plaster myself against the wall. I was forced to kneel with my other knee on the hard tiled floor, an issue most snails don't contend with. Overhead perched a flock of wrens and doves that would have been restless at all the commotion I caused, tipping off passersby, but they were frozen in time behind glass eyes and a glass wall. I was a genius. My knee would smart for some time, sure, but I was a genius.

Soon came the *clop-clop* of heavy shoes up the hall, but they seemed to be moving right-to-left, the wrong direction. I retreated farther into my shell, and then craned my neck backward to catch a curious glimpse of whoever walked my way with such casual authority. It was Sister Barbara, her leather soles echoing off plaster and glass like mule shoes in a granite canyon. For one brief moment I saw her as she was, relaxed in her gate, ambling forward with neither joy nor anger, a wet Kleenex bunched in her hand.

Sister Barbara had walked the halls of St. Génevière's for nearly two decades, and she had overcome any mild curiosity she may have felt over the boxes' contents years ago. She was not a vain woman in need of a mirror, so I will never understand why she chose to pivot her head at the precise moment I was most visible. A step sooner or later, and all she would have seen would have been a giant Japanese salamander or a ruby-throated hummingbird. Instead she saw me.

I have always believed that God and I were friends. I know I've done things that have really wrinkled his forehead, but I don't think he's mean. As close as we might get though, I don't think he'll ever let me get away with something I shouldn't. Not for long, anyway. Sister Barbara had been strolling up the hall, probably to fetch my class. She might have been thinking about daffodils or meat loaf or a dress she wore when she was a little girl—just minding her own business—when God himself grabbed her by the nostrils and yanked her head to the left.

Or maybe, on the first day of school, my mom gave her a bottle of pills and a note saying, "Take one pill each morning with a glass of water in order to read Timothy's mind. It works for me."

Heart of a Lamb: A Few Thoughts
from Herman Meier

I like bugs. I mean I *really* like bugs. I can hear my mom now: *Herman Emerson Meier, just because you like bugs doesn't mean everyone else does. And I can assure you that not everyone wants to hear about them!* That's what she'd say if she was here, but since she's not, let me tell you about bugs. I can't say for sure, but I'll bet Timmy Larkin likes bugs.

Ever let a bug crawl on you? Sometimes it happens when you're sleeping, and maybe you wake up, but lots of times you don't. Especially if you're in that deep REM sleep when your dreams are really chugging and your eyeballs fly around your head like somebody let go of a pair of balloons. Bugs come out at night because that's when you're usually sleeping and they don't want to get caught. Dentists tell you to brush your teeth after every meal, and especially before you go to bed, and they say it's because brushing your teeth'll help prevent cavities. But there's another reason, too. See, bugs don't like the smell of toothpaste, but they do like the smell of just about everything else we stick in our mouths. Once I forgot to throw away my lunch leftovers, and when I came back a couple hours later, there were ants all over. The proof, like my grandma says, was in the pudding.

Bad as that sounds, you go to sleep without brushing your teeth, you might as well put a sign on your chin that says *Free Supper Served Anytime Between Now And Sunup!* You'll have bugs crawling all over you from here to Christmas, and there you'll be, probably dreaming you turned into a crowded beach or a highway at rush hour, or maybe the dirt floor at a barn dance. And when bugs catch you with your mouth hanging open, they walk right in like they own the place. Once I

25

read in a science magazine that the average American swallows a pound of bugs a year while sleeping.

I know a lot about bugs. For instance, did you know that tapeworms come from fleas? That's why cats get them so much. Cats don't take baths like most people do; they lick themselves all over instead. Then they throw up all the dirt and hair they swallowed. Problem is, sometimes they swallow fleas, too. And when a flea ends up in your stomach, where everything is all warm and cozy, it never wants to leave. So when a cat starts heaving, the flea grabs on to whatever's nailed down, and it rides out the storm until all the dirt and hair and barf whoosh by. Oh, the cat's stomach juices'll kill the flea sooner or later, but that's not as good as it sounds. Its little flea body melts like an m&m, and sometimes a tapeworm egg falls out. A flea's bad. Tapeworm's worse.

The egg hatches, and out pops a little tapeworm head. The head has little hooks on it, and they latch onto your intestinal wall like a picture of your Aunt Gladys that's really scary but you have to keep it up anyway in case she ever stops by. Then it hangs there and gobbles up bits of cat food, growing little slimy body segments like how a rattlesnake grows rattles. Pretty soon the tapeworm's miles long, and the cat's walking around all skinny and sick as a dog. And it can happen to you, too, if you go licking cats.

So you see, I like science. I don't really like math because it's just numbers. And reading's just words. I don't really like reading about science either, unless whatever I'm reading about is sitting in front of me so I can put my hands on it. That's why I don't really enjoy reading about planets or earthquakes. I've never touched a planet, except the one I'm standing on, and that doesn't really count. But I do like playing with bugs and doing experiments with chemicals and fire. Once Sister Glenda set a paper towel on fire and jammed it in a milk bottle. Then she crammed a shelled hard-boiled egg into the mouth of the bottle. The fire went out and the bottle filled up with smoke. Then there was a loud *POP!* and the egg got sucked into the bottle. That was a pretty good day. Another time she took us outside and showed us how we can focus sunlight through a magnifying glass onto a leaf and set it on fire. First there was a tiny dot of gold light on the leaf, then smoke, then the whole leaf burst into flames.

Fire changes things. I can remember Sister Glenda telling us things can't really be destroyed. They can be broken, smashed to smithereens, but they can't be completely destroyed. Even if you set something on fire, like a newspaper or a GI Joe, it might turn into something else—a pile of ashes or a blob of orange plastic goop—but you just can't make it go away. Part of what's burning floats off into the air as smoke, and it might blow far away, but it never *goes* away. It always ends up someplace. Thousands and thousands of candles have been lit in that chapel in Italy, the one with the naked Bible pictures on the ceiling, and then people noticed all kinds of soot stuck to the painting. That's where the smoke from all the candles went. It stuck to the ceiling. It just took hundreds of years for anyone to spot it.

When I was little I was roasting marshmallows with my cousins, and 'my coat sleeve caught fire. My uncle tackled me and rolled me in the dirt like how my mom flops chicken parts around in flour, and pretty soon the flames were gone. But I had burns all over my arm from my wrist to my elbow, and I had to stay in the hospital for a week. When they finally took the bandages off, my arm looked like a candy bar somebody left on the dashboard of a car. It wasn't all oozy, but it did look like it melted and then dried funny. Some nurses helped me learn how to move my arm again and how to keep it clean. I can't throw a ball with it, but that's just because I can't throw a ball. I'll never have any hair on it like my dad's, and it doesn't sweat like my other arm does, but it works pretty good now. I can even write with it and color with it. Ever since it happened though, people have treated me different. At first they all did everything for me, like putting my shoes on my feet or cutting my food, because they were afraid I might break. Now they think I'm contagious, like their arms might melt too, if they touch mine. So you see, fire changes things.

I'm not afraid of fire though, like you'd think. I'm more afraid of coats. And cats, but I've already said why. I like the way fire spreads and takes over. You wad up a paper towel and ignite one corner, and in a few seconds the whole thing lights up. Then the flames pass away as quickly as they came, leaving a smoky ball of ash with tiny orange glowworms writhing on its surface. It's hypnotic, especially at night. Don't get me wrong; I'm not a pyromaniac. I don't go around setting things on fire, but if there's a good fire burning, I might stand there and watch it for a few minutes.

There's one thing I won't do with fire though, and it has to do with bugs. Once I saw some bad kids on my street doing the magnifying glass experiment on a beetle they caught. They'd knocked the beetle around pretty good, and he couldn't get off his back. While he lay there kicking his feet in the air, the bad kids tried to set his chest on fire. There weren't any flames, but I'll bet it really hurt. I should know. I wanted to stop those bad kids, but I wasn't strong enough.

It's hard being the smallest kid in class, and the weakest. And that's before you have a melted arm. Timmy Larkin is actually the smallest kid in class, even though he doesn't think so, but he doesn't have a melted arm. We take turns being picked last for stuff. It usually depends what we're being picked for. If we're playing kickball at recess, I get picked last because I sometimes trip over the ball when I try to kick it. Besides, Timmy can run really fast. But if we're playing a game where you have to be quiet and pay attention, Timmy always gets picked last. He can kick a ball, and he can run, but he can't be quiet or pay attention for anything.

We're pretty good friends, me and Timmy. Well, sometimes we are. He doesn't pick on me like some of the other kids do, like David and Richard or Martha and Nina. He sometimes picks on me, but not always. The other kids pick on him too, and when that happens, we're friends. One day a big third grader named Curt Ricker knocked Timmy's books out of his hands when we were in the library. Timmy had a bunch of butterfly books he wanted to show that Dorazio girl he's always talking about. He'd just got up the guts to talk to her when Ricker slapped the books out of his hands. Then there was a lot of laughing. I could see Timmy kneeling on the floor, scooping up his books and peeking at the Dorazio girl, trying to see if she was one of the kids laughing. Then he looked at me, but I didn't laugh. I've learned that sometimes a melted arm isn't the worst thing that can happen to you.

A weird thing happened one day in Sister Glenda's science class. She took us downstairs to the science lab, which was on the way to Sister Helga's music room, just off the hall with all the frozen animals. It was my favorite room in the whole school. There were beakers and vials and test tubes and hoses and sinks all over. I didn't know what any of it was for, but it looked like a mad scientist worked there. Maybe he could make a giant terrarium, built from the biggest fish tank he could find, and he could fill it with dirt and ferns and rocks. Then he could jam it full of bugs from all over the world. He could have scorpions and spiders and beetles and mantids. And he could have a name for each one.

So anyway, Sister Glenda told us about all the different branches of science, and as she did, she passed examples of each around the room. For geology she had a geode, which was a rock as big as a potato. It was cut in half, and even though it was just an ordinary-looking rock on the outside, it was stuffed with hundreds of purple crystals on the inside. When she told us about chemistry, she poured some vinegar into a bowl with baking soda, and it bubbled up and over. That was great. She showed us leaves for biology and she dropped lead balls onto carbon paper for physics, and she had a barometer for meteorology. I didn't understand anything she said about barometric pressure, but I stopped thinking about it completely when she introduced zoology and pulled out her last item: a lamb's heart.

I had eaten lamb before, with mint jelly on Easter, and I had gobbled turkey and chicken and cow and pig. I've always wondered why people are sometimes sensitive about what they call their food—you don't eat cow, you eat *beef*; you don't eat pig, you eat *pork*—but when you're eating a chicken, you're eating *chicken*. Same with lamb. But when a lamb grows up and turns into lunch, it's called *mutton*. I've even seen the lamb chops before they've been put on the grill, and they don't bother me. It's all just meat. But I'll never forget that lamb's heart.

It was smaller than I thought it would be, about the size of a ping-pong ball. I thought it would be all bloody, but it wasn't. In fact, floating there in a jar of formaldehyde, it looked like a huge piece of beige gum somebody chewed up and rolled into a ball. I was glad to be last in line that day, because I didn't want to let go of it. It was so still. I wondered about what happened to the rest of the lamb. I looked around the room, but I didn't see it anywhere. It must have been far away. I thought about how lonely the lamb must've been without its heart. Then I realized I was holding more than just the lamb's heart; I was holding its whole life. There just wasn't anything else left.

It made me think about Timmy and his books, and me and my arm. I wondered if the lamb would feel sorry for us, but I decided it probably wouldn't. Even though we had problems, we had done more and seen more and laughed more in our lives than that poor lamb ever got to. And as long as the carpool got us home and back, there'd always be another day for us to walk around with our hearts.

By the way, I also have allergies, which actually gives me more problems than my arm. My arm only gives me problems when somebody else looks at it, but my allergies are another story. One time though, it was a pretty funny story.

I'm allergic to dust, chlorine bleach, perfume, certain kinds of soap, and plants of all kinds. I also have to stay away from cats, but that's OK because at least I'll never catch tapeworms. My nose runs like an Olympic sprinter, my eyes water, and you never know which one of my nostrils will work when I wake up. Half the time, when my nostrils do work, I get those whistle boogers, which almost makes it all worth it. You breathe in, and it sounds like you have a meadowlark up your nose. Which is even better than having a flapper. Flappers are those boogers you get that open and shut when you breathe like they're on a hinge. Like a screen door on a windy day.

And there's another good thing about having allergies: I discovered a long time ago I can make myself sneeze by pressing the sharp edge of my fingernail against my upper lip and scratching my front teeth with it. It works like magic—press, scratch, sneeze—every time. When I showed Timmy, he came up with a really great idea.

I always ended up sitting by Nina Campbell more often than anybody should have to. She was never very nice to me, and more than once she acted like she might shrivel up like a raisin if I touched her. I sat in front of her in homeroom, next to her in math, and behind her in religion. One day Timmy told me to start sneezing the moment she sat down. Real sneezes, with lots of snot and spray that everyone could see. And I'd need to pile up bunches of wet Kleenexes on my desk and breathe loud through my mouth. "But be sure to stop if one of you ever gets up and moves around the room," Timmy said.

It didn't take too long before somebody suggested I was allergic to Nina. I think it was Martha McRory who thought of it first, after I'd sneezed twenty or thirty times. Sister Barbara didn't know what to do. People just don't get allergic to each other, and it wasn't like Nina was wearing perfume or anything. Timmy was sitting on the front row when all this was going on, and he raised his hand and offered to trade places with me. Normally Sister Barbara liked to have Timmy sit where she could keep an eye on him, but I was causing such a commotion that she agreed to it. Nina was starting to get a little worried about herself, like maybe she was as freaky as she thought I was.

Of course, once Timmy got parked next to Nina, he couldn't just sit there and behave himself. Picking on her was one of his favorite things to do. He'd run through her hop-scotch game during recess. During lunch he'd open his mouth real wide and show her what he was chewing, and if he ever got in front of her in line he'd stop dead so she'd run into him. Once he told me to give him the next toad I caught because he wanted to hide it in her lunch or drop it down her jacket hood. He was always doing stuff to her. It was almost like he liked her or something.

Long time ago Timmy taught himself to sneeze by rolling up the corner of a Kleenex like a snake and sliding it up his nose. He hadn't been sitting beside Nina for two minutes before he started sneezing with the same soggy violence I'd been. His sneezes were huge, like something out of a mammoth, and there were buckets of mucous, just like I like it. But Sister Barbara saw what he was up to with the Kleenex and she shipped him back up front. She replaced him with Cheryl Diorio, who sort of just stared at the scratches on her desk and nibbled her fingers.

That was my favorite moment at St. Génevière's. For a few minutes I had a good friend, I had used my gifts and talents to get a couple laughs—instead of falling on my face or dropping my tray in the lunchroom—and I got the best of Nina Campbell. I'd forgotten all about my arm, and for a minute there, I didn't even mind my allergies. It was a pretty good day.

Hockenberry Farm

There were five Hockenberrys at St. Géneviève's, and they all had chin dimples and a funny little sticker-weed of hair that stuck up off the back of their heads. My Grandma Larkin told me those are called cowlicks because it looks like a cow snuck up behind them and went *blaaaap!* against the backs of their heads. This made sense to me because the Hockenberrys owned a dairy farm a few miles south of St. Géneviève's. What a creative way to wash your hair!

Andrew Hockenberry and I were in the same grade. He didn't talk much, but once in the lunchroom he squeaked out a gasser that people were still talking about an hour later in Sister Ricarda's religion class. At first I thought he was scooting his hands across the table, sort of the way a girl's leg squeaks on her chair. But when I looked at his hands, they weren't moving. The noise kept building, and by the time I looked at his face I knew what he was doing. He was listing to one side like a torpedoed gunboat, and he appeared to be gazing right through my head at the table behind me. The noise cut out for just an instant, then he scrunched his eyes real tight and it started again. This time it came in lower, like the bassoon in that Russian musical about the disobedient boy and the wolf. He revved it up an entire octave and finished with a sharp sputter, like a chunk of chewed sausage shot through a straw. He didn't look to us for affirmation but continued with his lunch, calm in his self-assurance that he was a master. Clark and I couldn't say a word; we just gaped at him as he ate his PB&J under the warm glow of our utmost respect.

(Andrew would never admit it, but it's possible that final *pop!* pushed out a bit more than just wind.)

Andrew had twin younger brothers, Joseph and Anthony, in kindergarten with Charlie. They looked exactly the same, with their sticker-weed cowlicks and chin dimples. There were also two Hockenberry sisters who had class beyond the kindergarten room in the east wing, but I didn't know their names. I always thought they were pretty, even though everyone called them *Big Frog* and *Bigger Frog*. There were some things at St. Géneviève's I just couldn't figure out.

One chilly autumn morning as the oaks and maples were beginning to slip into their evening wear, we took a field trip to Hockenberry Farm. It was a rare opportunity to wear sneakers to school instead of our good shoes. There was a thin fog along the way that made the trees lining the road look like they were hiding behind tracing paper. It was cold enough for jackets, but the sun was trying its best to warm things up. By the time we got to the farm, most of the fog had burned off, and it felt like we might get to walk around in our shirtsleeves after lunch.

The Hockenberrys lived in a large yellow house on the edge of the farm. It wasn't lemon yellow; it was pale, like butter. It was old, but in a good way. Comfortable, like old jeans or sneakers. It didn't look like the houses you see sprouting up in new neighborhoods these days. Granddad Larkin would say the all-American porch was tailor-made for sipping lemonade and listening to a baseball game on the radio. A border of holly bushes grew like a prickly green mote just off the edge of the porch. If there had been snow on the ground, it would have felt like a field trip right into a Christmas card. Andrew told me one of his sisters had pushed him off the porch once, and he had ended up with little pinpricks all over himself.

He did more talking on the bus ride over than I had ever heard out of him before. He had gotten a Hot Wheels garage and racetrack for his birthday and hoped to show it off. But when the bus rolled past the house, pulled into a dirt lot by the barn, and parked next to a colossal orange tractor, Sister Barbara made us all button up for instructions. Then Andrew clammed up like the kid we all knew. It must be pretty rough to go on a school field trip to your own house and be told where to go and what to do by someone who doesn't even live there.

Mr. Hockenberry stepped out of the barn and greeted us when we got off the bus. He didn't look anything like my dad, who wears a tie to work every day. Mr. Hockenberry wore green coveralls and looked dirtier than even I sometimes get. He laughed and said he had been playing with the cows. I liked Mr. Hockenberry right away. He was the first grown up I had ever met who didn't mind getting filthy. I started wondering about some of the things my mom had taught me, stuff like: *Good boys take a bath every day* and *You should always wash your hands after touching an animal.*

He told us how he had to get up hours before sunrise every day and take care of the cows. Then he led us into the barn to show us what that meant. There was a whole herd of black and white cows in there, standing side-by-side and nose-to-nose like a parking lot full of fuzzy police cars. Mr. Hockenberry showed us how we could tell they were cows—instead of bulls—by their udders. I had seen pictures, but it wasn't until I got up close that I noticed how repulsive an udder is, all muddy and covered with veins and scraggly hairs. Each udder had a bunch of hoses connected to it, and all the hoses bunched together and ran into a huge silver machine at the end of the barn. The whole operation looked like a giant metallic squid had seized a herd of cows by the udders and was dragging them off to an all-night diner.

Mr. Hockenberry told us the hoses were drawing milk out of the cows, then he reached under the closest cow and pulled off a hose to show us where the milk actually came from. He told us he had to attach all those hoses every morning, and then come back later in the day and take them all off. I asked him if the cows ever got bored just standing there all day long, and he told me that cows are born bored. "But being cows," he said, "they aren't smart enough to do anything about it, so they just stand around being bored."

I could understand that. Sometimes I get bored. Sometimes I'll ask my dad a question, and twenty minutes later he's still giving me the answer.

Yawn. Be careful what you ask a science enthusiast.

Once I asked Sister Glenda why we have seasons. She pulled out a globe and showed me about how the Earth spins like a top on what she called an *axis*. This axis, she said, is like a huge spear that runs from the North Pole, which is just past Canada, to the South Pole, which is somewhere beyond Australia. It's also tilted, so when the Earth whips around the sun, spinning as it goes, sometimes Canada gets all the sunshine—that's summer—and sometimes Australia gets all the sunshine—and that's winter.

"So the Earth is a giant marshmallow roasting on a stick," I said, "and it has to keep pitching and turning so it doesn't burn up."

I'd figured it out. But then she went on and on about a tropical jet stream and solstices and I don't remember what else. The very next day I asked her why pigs like mud, and with wild eyes and sweeping gestures she told the class all about sweat glands and evaporation and why dogs pant. By the time she was done, I couldn't even remember what I had asked her. They say people who ask questions are intelligent. That might be, but people who ask *certain* people questions means *some* people never learn. I asked Mr. Hockenberry why pigs like mud, and he told me they wouldn't be pigs if they didn't. I liked his answer better than Sister Glenda's, even though I didn't know any more about pigs than I had before.

I missed everything else Mr. Hockenberry said about why the cows were lined up with hoses on their udders because frankly, I don't like the way milk sticks to the back of your mouth. I think I would've paid more attention if cows gave root beer. Which gave me an idea:

Rooty, the Root Beer Cow
by Timothy N. Larkin

Once upon a time there was a root beer cow, so called because she gave root beer instead of milk. Her closest friends called her Rooty, and so will we.

Rooty didn't come into the world the way most cows do. I don't know how most cows are born, but however it happens, it wasn't the way Rooty was born. You see, Rooty hatched from an Easter egg. Farmer Brown and his wife, Mrs. Brown, had an Easter egg hunt for their fifteen kids. All the kids were twins, even though there were fifteen of them instead of two. So when the kids were asleep, waiting for the Easter Bunny to come, Farmer and Mrs. Brown ran all over the farm hiding plastic Easter eggs filled with hard candy and jelly beans. (I know it was the Browns who hid the eggs because first graders don't believe in the Easter Bunny.)

The sun came up Easter Sunday morning, and after Farmer Brown was done hooking up his cows to the silver squid, he came in, ate breakfast and put on his Sunday clothes. He didn't take a bath first because he knew he was going to get dirty again later when he unhooked all his cows. That was OK, though, because Mrs. Brown didn't mind a little dirt, and besides, everyone knew Farmer Brown was a farmer. That's why they all called him Farmer Brown. Besides, Farmer was his first name.

While the Brown family sat in church listening to the preacher, a magpie swooped into their cornfield looking for trouble. He stood between two rows of corn and waved his bottom at the scarecrow. "You don't scare me!" the magpie said, "because I'm not a crow!" The scarecrow just stood there, its feelings too hurt for him to reply. "In fact," said the magpie, "I don't think you'd scare me even if I were a crow!" The scarecrow would've walked away like his mom had taught him to do when bullies come around, but he was stuck on a pole.

"Oh yeah?" said the scarecrow. (If you've read The Wizard of OZ, *you'd know that scarecrows don't have brains, so when confronted, all they can say is "Oh, yeah?" The scarecrow tried to spit on the magpie, but nothing came out of his mouth because his head was full of straw.)*

"I can do anything I want!" the magpie shouted, and he stomped all over the baby corn, which had just been growing there, not hurting anybody. The scarecrow got mad and told the magpie to cut it out, but the magpie refused. "What are you gonna do about it?" the magpie laughed. The scarecrow knew he couldn't do anything, so he stayed where he was, stuck on a pole.

The magpie noticed a small yellow Easter egg tucked between two tufts of corn, and he pecked at it with his beak. When the egg didn't break, the magpie scooped it up and tried to fly away with it. As he rose above the scarecrow's head, the magpie tried to tell the scarecrow how bored he was with him, but when he opened his mouth to speak, the egg fell out. (Magpies can talk a lot, but the stuff they say isn't as smart as they think it is). The egg bounced off the scarecrow (who again said, "Oh, yeah?") and it soft-landed in a thick pile of manure.

After church, when the Browns were enjoying their Easter egg hunt, three of the kids, Esther, Lester, and Chester, spotted the egg, but none of them wanted to pick it up. So the egg remained in the manure for a week. When the dung beetles came along to dismantle the manure and carry it home, they stood on the egg so they wouldn't get their feet dirty. As a result, the egg sank deeper into the manure until it was hardly visible at all. Then the rain came, and manure mud trickled into the egg and mixed with the stuff Farmer and Mrs. Brown had hidden inside, which, incidentally, was a piece of hard candy shaped liked a tiny root beer barrel. Even though the candy was wrapped in plastic, the mud mixed with it anyway.

Two days later, a pelican returning to the sea after visiting friends upstate saw the manure and flew in for a closer look. The beetles and the rain had worn down the manure so it resembled a small brown recliner. The pelican was tired, so he rested on it. His bottom must have been pretty warm, because a little while later, the egg hatched and out popped a miniature cow. The cow ran around the cornfield until she got big, then she decided she wanted to be like the other cows on the farm. She strolled into the barn one day, and when Farmer Brown hooked her up to the squid machine, all this root beer started running through the hose! It turned all the milk in the machine into root beer as well! People from all over came to Farmer Brown's farm to taste his root beer milk, and when people's moms went to the store, they bought Farmer Brown's Root Beer Milk, and they all lived happily ever after.

******

I was standing there thinking how great my story was when I realized I was the only person left in the barn. I ran outside to look for my class and saw them gathered by a fence some distance away. I was going to be mad at them for walking out and not leaving a message, but then I saw what they were looking at. Mr. Hockenberry was telling everyone how to ride a horse. And there was an actual horse standing there next to him. The thing was a monster. Mr. Hockenberry told us the horse's name was Elmer, and he talked about pulling left or right on something called a bridle to get him to turn, and he told us how to make him go and how to make him stop. Then he asked who wanted to be first to ride Elmer. I wanted to be first, but he picked Martha McRory. Martha always got picked first for everything. Sister Barbara said I had to go last because I had dawdled in the barn while everyone else had walked over to the corral.

Dawdle was one of those new words I sometimes heard but was afraid to ask about. I suspected it had something to do with walking like a duck, but I assure you that once I discovered where I was supposed to be, I ran to the corral in a way most ducks don't. Best not to argue, though.

Being last made me feel like Herman Meier, the smallest kid in the class. He was almost always picked last. Everyone said he threw worse than a girl, he always had crust under his nose, and once he dropped his tray in the dining room.

Mr. Hockenberry helped Nina Campbell get into the saddle, then he lifted me up and helped me get on behind her. Then he led Elmer twice around the corral. Nina had a rough time in school. She stuttered sometimes when she had to read aloud, and she needed all ten of her fingers to do math, but sitting behind her, I noticed her hair smelled pretty.

(I would point out that the wind blew her hair in my face. I don't want people to think I'm a hair-sniffer.)

Mr. Hockenberry pulled Elmer up to the gate at the end of our ride and told us if we wanted to ride any more, we'd need to put in another quarter. I thought that was funny, but Nina started looking through Elmer's mane for a slot. Then she remembered that she didn't have a quarter anyway.

After everyone rode Elmer, Sister Barbara led us back to the barn to wash our hands while Mr. Hockenberry locked the corral gate. While we were walking, I looked back at Elmer, who was busy huffing through his nostrils. What if there was a fire in the corral? How would Elmer get out if the gate was locked? It didn't occur to me that the only thing in the corral that could burn was the corral itself—nothing but a post and rail fence laid out in a square—and perhaps a bit of straw in one corner. So I looked after Elmer and I worried, which is why I didn't see the line of kids stop in front of me.

"Ouch!" Martha shouted when I smashed flat into her, but it sounded more like *Oukph!* because she in turn crashed into Nina, taking in a huge mouthful of Nina's curly red hair. I had stepped on the back of Martha's foot. Both girls wheeled and called me *Loser Larkin!* at the same time, like they had rehearsed it. And really, they had. Lots of times. I said I was sorry, but they were still mad at me, Martha with her sore foot and Nina with Martha-spit in her hair.

"What's all the commotion?" Sister Barbara demanded, storming to the back of the line.

"Sister Barbara, Timmy pushed me!" Martha shouted, using the familiar tone people always used when telling on me. They'd say the teacher's name first, then my name on a higher note. And it was always the same note. I discovered from my piano lessons that the space on the scale between *Sister Barbara* and *Timmy* was always what musicians call a Perfect Fourth—the same space that sits between *Here* and *comes the bride!* I paused to reflect on that phenomenon, trying to think of other songs that started with Perfect Fourths.

That's why "The Eyes of Texas" was playing in my head when Sister Barbara blocked the sun in front of me and shouted, *"Well?!"*

My first thought was something she herself had taught me about using the word *well* in writing. *A well's a hole in the ground, Sister!* I didn't say it, though. The truth is, I didn't know what to say because I hadn't heard the question. "Um, sorry?" was all I could think of. I've had occasional moments of brilliance in my day, but this wasn't one of them.

"We'll see if you're sorry," said Sister Barbara. "I want you to walk with me at the front of the line." Normally, getting to walk at the front of the line is a special privilege reserved for the good kids—your Nina types and your Martha types. It isn't so special, though, to have to walk at the front of the line holding hands with the teacher, especially one who always carries a wadded up Kleenex. My troubles continued when Sister Barbara let go of my hand near the barn to let the line pass. "Straight through that door, Timothy Larkin. And no monkeyshines!"

There was a door on the back of the cow barn that had what Grandma Larkin calls a Devil Doorknob. It turned both directions, the way normal doorknobs do, but it caught before the bolt cleared the doorframe. As a result, I turned the knob, pushed, and ran smack into the door. Then the rest of the line smashed into me. Again there was a commotion, again there was telling, again with the familiar Perfect Fourth, and again there was a wadded up Kleenex in my hand. And I had to sit next to Sister Barbara while we ate lunch. Then Martha and Nina called me Loser Larkin again. The all-too familiar clicks of dominoes.

We ate our lunches at a long picnic table on the back-side of the house. Andrew asked if he could take some of us up to his room, but his mom said no. At least that was better than Sister Barbara saying no. Mr. Hockenberry ate lunch with us, and when he was done he said if the rest of us finished in time, we could all go meet Old Variable. Andrew, who was sitting across the table from me, leaned over like he was going to make another squeak and whispered, "Maybe we'll get to see him pee." I didn't know who Old Variable was, but Andrew's enthusiasm told me I wouldn't want to miss it.

Sure, that sounds gross, but you need to understand that one of the most important things for a boy in elementary school is being recognized as the One Who Pees The Longest, even if you hold the title for only a day. And although you tend to lose interest in that sort of thing by the time you grow up, it's a gentlemanly sport where worthy opponents are held in high regard. Clark and I stuffed the remains of our sandwiches into our lunchboxes and slammed them shut. We were ready.

Old Variable turned out to be an enormous bull with horns like sharpened baseball bats. He was caked with mud and he had red eyes and a surly attitude. My dad once told me a story about a guy named Theseus, who went down into a gigantic stone maze and killed the Minotaur, a greasy monster with the body of a man and the head of a bull. Looking at Old Variable with his enormous cranium, I couldn't understand how a Minotaur could walk around with a bull head without tipping over.

Maybe it didn't walk around at all. Old Variable sure didn't. He just stood there, staring at us through the fence rails.

Once in a while he'd burp, and then he'd chew for a little while like he had bubble gum. Clark could only whisper, "This is gonna be good."

And it didn't take too long for Old Variable to give over, as Great-Grandma Larkin used to say. He let go with a snort and the earth beneath him exploded with the mighty sound of rushing waters. Clark and I called Andrew, who had wandered away moments earlier. Old Variable was still producing by the time Andrew returned to the fence. "You could've gone to the sty for a look at the hogs and he'd still be going," Andrew informed us. We stood in silent wonder at the outflow in the same way Dr. Goddard must have stood as he test-fired his first rocket engine.

Sister Barbara called after us, rolling her eyes at the things that amuse young boys. Dragging our feet, we shambled onto the bus for the ride back to St. Géneviève's. In all, the trip was successful. We learned where milk comes from and where it goes before it gets to the fridge. We got to ride a horse. Even though I wasn't on Elmer for very long, my legs still felt a little like they'd been straddling a barrel. Finally we got to meet Old Variable, and we got to see him give over. Both the force and the duration staggered our young minds. Mr. Hockenberry could've hooked Old Variable up to a generator and powered a small grocery store through April. It was the highlight of the trip.

Sister Beryl's Candy Columns
(Charlie's Story)

Want to know one thing I can never understand about Timmy? Timmy.

I don't know. People always ask Mom and Dad if we we're twins. Seeing as I look like him, I oughtta be able to figure him out. And I probably oughtta be learning from him, seeing as he's older and everything. But when I see him do things, lots of times all I can think is *Oh, Timmy.* Or sometimes even *Nooo, Timmy!*

Like one day, when Mom and Dad were at this meeting or something? It was just before Christmas. Maybe they were shopping. Anyway, so me and Timmy got to stay after school and play in my room. Well, OK, *Sister Beryl's* room, not mine. Sister Beryl was my kindergarten teacher.

It was great. Sister Beryl had bunnies and even a baby sheep. I mean, real bunnies and a real baby sheep! It was funny because whenever we were supposed to take a nap, just when everybody was asleep, sometimes the sheep would say *Baaaa!* and we'd all laugh until Sister Beryl said *SsssT!* She never said Shh! It was always *SsssT!* With a great big T at the end, like if she was trying to blow a piece of fuzz or something off her tongue. She was like that with everything. She didn't say cookies, she called them *cookinies.* She was always saying stuff like that. But when she gave you a hug it felt like a big happy cloud wrapped around you.

My room—I mean Sister Beryl's room—was really big. It was like two whole rooms put together, but without any walls in the middle. She had big paper pictures of mountains and baby lions and elephants all over the walls. Her desk was over by the window so she could look out and see the trees.

45

Then there were chairs and two big round tables where we could color. There were bright red shelves under the window where she kept all her stuff. She had puzzles, a ton of books about animals and planets, and she even had a bees' nest on a stick.

There were four big poles in the middle of the room. But they were fat poles. Not like flagpoles. These poles were so huge I couldn't even hug one of them and touch my fingers. They made a square on the floor, and in the middle Sister Beryl had a rug with the whole world on it. There were mats on the floor on the other side of the room. That's where we took our naps. Sometimes, when I wasn't sleepy, I'd lie on my tummy with my chin on the floor. There was a heater under the windows, and sometimes I'd look at the dust underneath. That was the only place where there was dust in Sister Beryl's room. It was like the dust knew it wasn't allowed to come out from under the heater.

Anyway, like I said, it was just before Christmas. Sister Beryl had one of those round paper Santa Clauses that you open up—sort of like a Christmas card or a book or something?—then you tape the ends together. She had it on her shelf next to the bees' nest. Sister Beryl said she had a brother and he made this thing called a Navy Scene, but instead of battleships it had cows and shepherds and Baby Jesus. They were all in this little garage made of twigs with grass on top. There was a Christmas tree, too, over by the door by the yellow steps where they had that big black metal bell. We helped decorate it—the tree, not the bell—with stuff we made out of construction paper and paste. And finally Sister Beryl took long pieces of red paper and wrapped them around the poles so they looked like great big candy canes. I don't know how she got the paper all the way to the ceiling, because I don't think it would've been a good idea for Sister Beryl to stand on a chair. She was real nice, but she would've squashed a chair.

When me and Timmy got the whole room to ourselves I was gonna build puzzles and pet the bunnies. You're not supposed to stick your finger in a bunny cage because they always think it's a carrot or something, and they might bite your finger. But these were nice bunnies. There was this big girl named Lisa who was gonna watch us. She wasn't big like Sister Beryl, but she was big, like in eighth grade. I bet she wishes she went home on the bus that day instead of staying with me and Timmy. I wonder if she got in trouble, too.

But instead of petting the bunnies, Lisa asked us if we wanted to color, and we said yes. First we put our coats on the hooks by the door. Then we went over to the round tables and got crayons. Timmy wanted to sit at his own table, but Lisa wouldn't let him. She wasn't mad, though. I drew a camel and Timmy drew a car he saw on TV. Then he stuck a crayon in the pencil sharpener. I said to him, "Timmy, we don't stick crayons in the pencil sharpener." Then he wanted to get scissors and cut out his car picture, but Lisa said she thought it would be better if she cut out the car. But she wasn't mad.

Timmy got mad, though. He said, "My mom lets me use the scissors at home." Lisa said, "Little boys shouldn't use the scissors when their moms aren't around," and I kind of knew what she meant. She didn't say little boys shouldn't use the scissors; she just said they shouldn't use the scissors when their moms aren't around. But Timmy started looking for the scissors anyway. He dumped the pencils all over the floor and then he didn't pick them up. He just went looking for the scissors some more. He came over to me and asked me if I knew where Sister Beryl keeps the scissors and I said probably in her desk. Then I looked at Lisa and it looked like she wished I hadn't told Timmy where the scissors were.

Timmy ran over to Sister Beryl's desk, but Lisa got there first and stood in his way. She wasn't mad, though. She just said that Timmy oughtta wait 'til Mom got there. Then he could use the scissors. I liked Lisa. She had a round face like the moon and she smiled a lot. She had long hair and she looked like she could be your big sister. And she looked like she wouldn't spank anyone. Timmy threw his car picture at her and almost hit her in the head with it. But she didn't get mad.

It was funny, what she did. She made her face all scary so you could see her teeth and she yelled real loud like a bear and grabbed Timmy's arms. I think he thought she was going to give him a spanking because he screamed and said, "Put me down!" but she only wanted to tickle him. Which is what she did. She put him on the floor and stuck her knee on his chest and tickled him. He laughed so hard I thought he was gonna do a b-m in his pants. Then she said, "I'm sorry but I can't give you the scissors. You'll have to wait until your mom gets here."

Now even though Timmy's real real smart, he's always doing something real real dumb. But actually this time he did something smart. He said, "Well, can *you* cut out my car picture please?" And Lisa told him yes, that was a good idea. Like if she hadn't thought of it already. Timmy was breathing real hard when Lisa went to go get the scissors, and I've seen him when he gets that way before. People think he's tired, but what he's doing is thinking about what he can do next. Lisa cut out the car picture, but Timmy yelled when she didn't cut out the smoke coming out the back of the car.

"You didn't cut out the smoke!" he said.

Really, I just thought it was a scribble, but I guess it coulda been smoke. Then Lisa said she was sorry and you could tell she meant it. Some people, when they say they're sorry, they don't really mean it. And sometimes when my mom makes Timmy say he's sorry, I don't listen 'cause I don't think it's really sorry if you don't mean it. And you never mean it when someone else makes you say it. But you could tell Lisa was sorry 'cause her mom wasn't around to make her say it.

I think Timmy was absent that day in church when they talked about forgiving and stuff, which is when you say it's OK after somebody tells you they're sorry. He said he'd never get to decorate the Christmas tree, and he went over and kicked one of the poles and all the stripes came off it. Then it didn't look like a candy cane any more. It just looked like a pole. Which is what it was, but it wasn't supposed to look like it. It needed to look like a candy cane.

Lisa made him sit down, but I don't think she was mad. She just didn't want him to kick any more poles. Then she cut out the smoke and got some tape and taped it to the car so it looked like it had smoke coming out. Then she helped me cut out my camel.

Timmy jumped out of his chair and said he was an airplane. He stuck his arms out and ran all around the room and he scared the sheep. He pretended he was shooting the sheep and he made machine gun noises. Then he ran by another pole and hit it with his hand and all its stripes fell off, too. Lisa ran over and grabbed him again, but this time she didn't tickle him. She scooped him up like the way my mom carries a bunch of dirty towels, and she carried him over to the table and asked him to sit next to her. She wasn't mad, though. She just wanted him to help her stick a hook made out of a silver pipe cleaner onto the back of his car, because she figured out that he wanted to hang the car on the Christmas tree. When she was putting his car on the tree (and he said he wanted it to be at the top, but she said, no, the angel had to go there, but maybe it could go underneath the angel) he ripped my camel's head off. For no good reason.

Lisa asked Timmy why he ripped my camel's head off and he said something about a cow and then they had an argument, but Lisa didn't get mad. She just made Timmy sit in a chair. I was mad, though. I wanted Timmy to get a spanking. But Lisa made everything OK when she helped me draw another camel. I think Timmy said something like how my camel looked like a cow. *You* try drawing a camel, I should've said. But Lisa could really draw a camel. It even looked like a camel, like the kind you see in pictures. Sister Beryl could've put it on her wall, but Lisa asked me if she could keep it after I colored it. She really did! (Don't tell anybody, but one day after I grow up, me and Lisa are getting married.)

Then Timmy ran over to the Christmas tree and took his car off the tree and told Lisa she could have his car, too. Lisa told him thank you, that was very sweet, but before Timmy could say you're welcome he was flying around the room scaring the baby sheep again. Then he hit another pole and watched all its stripes fall off. And all I could think of was *Nooo, Timmy.* Like I told you.

Lisa chased after him and he yelled "Enemy fighter! Enemy fighter!" and he shot his guns at her. She caught him over by the bunnies and told him she was going to have to tell Mom and Dad. She said she wished she didn't have to, but she said people would wonder what happened to the poles. Timmy said he was sorry, and he went over to the table and drew a dinosaur eating a camel. And I think he was sorry, but before Mom and Dad got there, he'd hit all four poles and squashed the paper Santa Claus. Like I said, I've seen Timmy before when he gets that way. And even though he knows Mom and Dad always find out, it never scares him 'til they do. So even though he's pretty smart, that's why he's so dumb.

Sister Beryl's Candy Columns
(Timothy's Story)

People always ask Mom and Dad if Charlie and I are twins. Can you believe that? I mean *look* at us! I'm obviously older, and I don't have a rope of snot hanging out of my nose like he usually does. OK, so he doesn't really walk around all day with a snoogy-snake hanging from his nose, but when he looks up at the sky, you can usually see a jumbo yellow wad hiding up one of his nostrils like a blob of predatory pancake batter, lurking in some dark alley, waiting to pounce on some unsuspecting victim.

I don't know. He's a pretty good little brother, I guess. Mostly. Mom says there isn't a bad bone in his body. He catches toads and pets them. One day he caught one and stuck it in a terrarium he put together with Dad. He thought his pet wooly bear caterpillar needed company. The toad liked the terrarium, but things didn't work out as well for the caterpillar. He does dumb stuff, Charlie, but it's little-kid dumb stuff. Like once in the middle of winter, when everything was all wet and slushy, I caught him eating chocolate chips off the grocery store floor. GROSSery store... Get it?!

But most of the time he's pretty smart for a dumb kid. He started kindergarten at St. Génevieve's when I was in first grade, but by the time I was in third grade at Valley View Elementary (where kids don't wear ties), he got bumped up to third grade too! That's another story, though. Why we were ever at Valley View is also a different story. You'll hear that one later. This is a story about his kindergarten room, but I'm kind of the star of it.

One Friday afternoon in December my mom and dad had a meeting with Sister Barbara and Sister Gwendolyn about my pills. They kept telling me over and over that I wasn't in trouble, but why else would they have a meeting with Sister Gwendolyn? I warned them about her, about how she kept monkey heads on a rope in her desk drawer, but they didn't listen. And it's because they didn't listen that I got in the biggest trouble of my life.

Charlie and I had to wait for them in Sister Beryl's kindergarten room. At first it was great. Sister Beryl's room was almost twice the size of Sister Barbara's, and it was crammed with all kinds of things that could almost make you forget you were in school. She had a wooden hutch that held a pair of floppy-eared rabbits, and she kept a sheep—an actual, real-life *sheep*—in a pen in the corner. She also had an empty hornet's nest the size of a volleyball on one of her shelves.

It was just before Christmas, and Sister Beryl had decorations all over the room. Most of them had been made by her students over the years. There were reindeer made of popsicle sticks, paper snowflakes taped to the windows, and a big paper maché Nutcracker. Charlie said it was named after a Russian belly dancer. Right next to that was a wooden Nativity scene big enough for a GI Joe to stand up in. It was said that Sister Beryl's brother built the stable and carved the animals himself.

The room was so big it needed four columns to hold the ceiling up, and Sister Beryl had wrapped them in red streamer so they looked like candy canes for a giant. Standing in the center of that room, I felt like Charlie Bucket walking into Willie Wonka's Chocolate Factory. And we had it all to ourselves!

Well, we *almost* had the room to ourselves. Mom had gotten an eighth grader named Lisa to babysit us. She had long black hair, and I liked her right away. She looked like Valerie Dorazio. She was drawing a picture of the Christmas Star at one of the kiddy tables when we walked in, and she asked us to join her. So we hung up our coats, grabbed a couple boxes of crayons off the shelf, and sat on either side of her. At first I wanted a whole table to myself, but Lisa said no. Too much mess to clean up, she said. She had a point; besides, she smelled like flowers. And she didn't have any hair on her knuckles or anything.

She asked us what we wanted to draw, and Charlie told her he wanted to draw a camel like the little wooden one over in the Nativity scene. Clark Bernard and I had just discovered a TV show called Speed Racer, and we both thought the Mach 5 was the greatest car on the planet, with its retractable saw blades and remote control seagull. I drew the Mach 5. I didn't bother with the saw blades or the seagull, but I did include the bulletproof bubble glass and a plume of smoke billowing from the exhaust pipe. It turned out so well I figured it should be put on prominent display on top of Sister Beryl's Christmas tree. I had to cut it out first, though, and that's when all the trouble started.

Lisa wouldn't let me use the scissors. I guess she was afraid I'd cut my arm off. And yeah, I realize stuff like that's been known to happen. One day in science class, Herman Meier told us how a fox caught in a trap would chew its own leg off to escape. Martha McRory told him that was dumb, and said if Herman ever got caught in a trap, he might chew *his* leg off, but there was a good chance it would be the wrong leg. Then Sister Glenda told us that it really does happen sometimes. Then she made Martha apologize.

I think we all agree a Christmas tree would look tacky with an $8\frac{1}{2} \times 11$ sheet of paper on it, but I couldn't get Lisa to understand. She was getting mad, and anger can cloud a person's judgment—even if that person looks a lot like Valerie Dorazio. I knew if Sister Beryl was any kind of teacher at all, she would have scissors in her desk. So when Lisa leaned over for a closer look at Charlie's camel, I ran over to the desk to look for the scissors.

When I got there, though, Lisa was blocking the way. Wow! I spun my head back to the kiddy table, half expecting to see her still sitting there talking to Charlie. I'd never seen a person move that fast. It was like she was magic, and it was at that point that I first suspected her of being a witch. She told me I needed to wait for my mom to get there before I could use the scissors, and when she smiled, it looked like maybe she had gotten her dad to file her teeth into points. I wanted to scream, but I couldn't make the sound. So I threw my picture at her instead. Then she tried to kill me.

She yelled really loud, thunder rising from her bowels, and she grabbed me. I could feel her leopard claws digging into the flesh of my arms, and as blood dripped from my dangling hands and pooled on the floor, she shook me like a rag doll and threatened to gobble me up. She would've too, but ogre witches never like to eat the main course before their salad arrives. So she slammed me on the floor and poked and prodded at my ribs with her nails, leaving traces of cemetery dirt embedded in my skin. I was so terrified I laughed, and I almost had an accident. I would've too, if she hadn't stopped jumping up and down on my chest.

When I finally wore her out and she sat back down at the table, I asked her if she would cut out my Mach 5 for me. I figured she'd slice the paper with her filthy talons the way a condor might gut a woodchuck, but when I looked at her hands, they were sweet and pretty again—just like Valerie Dorazio's. She said she would be glad to cut out my Mach 5, and she got up and pulled a pair of kiddy scissors from Sister Beryl's desk drawer.

But she cut off the smoke! She might've been an eighth grader, but she wasn't a very bright one. I told her you can't have a Mach 5 on your Christmas tree without smoke coming out of it: everyone knows that. Then I stomped across the room. I was going to get my coat and leave, but when I got halfway to the coat rack, I felt the sudden urge to kick something. Usually I'm a thrower and a breaker, but sometimes when the situation calls for it, nothing fixes my problems like kicking something. The handiest object was one of Sister Beryl's candy columns, and when I kicked it, the most amazing thing happened. At first all I could think about was my aching toe, but then I noticed the streamer had torn where I kicked it, and the candy cane stripes had unraveled into one straight line down the side of the pole. I stood there for a moment just watching the streamer as it hung from its masking tape anchor, the way a spider dangles in midair. It was hypnotic.

Lisa got up out of her chair and stomped over to where I was—she was a pretty good stomper—then lashed out with one of her claws and grabbed me by the face. She had begun once again to look less like Valerie Dorazio and more like Sister Gwendolyn. In fact, she might have been Sister Gwendolyn's little sister, sent upstairs to spy on me while my parents were downstairs being eaten. It was a grave situation.

Lisa looked like she might dismember me for easier storage, so I went limp. Sister Glenda told me once that opossums do that when they think a puma is going to eat them. Pumas are a lot like Sister Gwendolyn: they like to feel their food wriggling all the way down their furry throats. They don't like to eat dead food. So I pretended I was dead. I even flopped my tongue out. Lisa dumped me onto a chair and told me to stay there for ten minutes.

As if a dead person could actually follow orders.

Sister Beryl's room had big windows, and as the winter afternoon sky gave way to dusk I could see the whole room reflected in the glass. I looked like a blond dot against the backdrop of columns and posters and assorted Christmas decorations. I waved, and my reflection waved back. I made fish lips, and my reflection responded in kind. When I stood up and stretched my arms like airplane wings, so did my reflection. I thought of Clark, my wingman, and I sensed what needed to be done. My squadron was in trouble, shot down over enemy territory and held captive by the hideous Sheep People of Arubaaaaa. I catapulted myself from the flight deck of my chair and screamed across the airy expanse of Sister Beryl's room.

As I neared the enemy headquarters, the Sheep Commander taunted me and said impolite things about my mother. Fortunately my machine guns had been armed with soap bullets earlier in the day, and now I vowed to wash his mouth out. My cannons blazed as I swooped low over enemy territory, but on my second swipe I was struck by ground fire. As I struggled to regain control of my craft, my wing clipped a nearby mountain and more streamer stripe fell—a thin red line bleeding from the clouds above.

I righted my plane and had just turned homeward when a wave of ape-bats appeared on my radar screen. They all had long, stringy black hair and they foamed at the mouth. Their leader slapped my fighter plane from the sky the way an angry kid might slap a light switch. And it had the same effect. I spiraled earthward, unconscious and unaware. I awoke in the Sheep People laboratory, heavily medicated and chained to an ape-bat foot soldier. She told me one false move and she'd ram a tape dispenser up my nose.

But then Lisa was pretty again, and I sat next to her as she taped a silver pipe cleaner to the back of my Mach 5. She had cut out the smoke and taped it in place while I had been engaged with the Sheep People. With its bulletproof glass and ferocious burst of exhaust, the car looked like it meant business. "Let's put it on the tree!" I told her. I wasn't as tall as Lisa, so it was agreed that she would place my Mach 5 on the tree. While she did so, I noticed a minor flaw in Charlie's camel: it looked like a cow.

I tried to explain to Charlie how camels have long necks, but he wouldn't listen to reason. I took it upon myself to show him, but when I reached for the picture, he pressed down with his fingers and the poor camel-cow-thing's head tore off. Quicker than a sneeze Lisa put her bear face back on and flung me across the room, where my broken body seeped into the cracks of the floor like spilled milk. If a cat had strolled by at that moment, I might have been lapped up and forgotten. For the first time that evening, I was genuinely frightened for my life.

Meanwhile, back at the kiddy table, Lisa helped Charlie draw another camel. When they were done, she asked him to sign the picture and she would keep it forever. I had recomposed myself by that point, and as I stood next to the hutch trying to see if one of the rabbits would eat a crayon, I could see that Lisa meant well. She really was beautiful, even prettier than Valerie Dorazio, and I decided I would marry her if she could ever get that face-changing habit under control. I granted her my Mach 5 as a peace offering, then I flew around the room in a reverie of romance.

My celebration was short-lived, however, when a squadron of Venusian viper-planes intercepted me and drove me headlong into a galactic space squid, which spewed toxic ropes of red streamer into the solar wind. Disoriented and bleeding into my flight suit, I sent out a distress signal. *"M'aidez! M'aidez!"* I cried, which is French for *May-day, May-day!* I don't know what that means, but fighter pilots always say it when they need someone to help them. "Enemy fighters! Enemy fighters!" But it was no good. My communications system was down, and in a swirl of dull light and dazzling darkness, I plummeted through the soupy Venusian atmosphere to my fiery demise.

Shortly after my remains washed up on the shore of a remote Venusian island, my parents escaped Sister Gwendolyn's treacherous tar pit and made their way above ground. When they emerged from the woods on that Venusian beachhead, they startled a ravenous black-haired tongue-troll picking through my bones. The oily creature addressed my parents in a familiar tone, and my fears that they might be lulled into dropping their guard were realized as my mom reached into her bio-belt and presented the troll a ten-dollar bill. The troll ate the bill the way I used to eat Tootsie Rolls—paper and all—then planted a death smooch on my skull. My dad, unmoved by my decomposed carcass, scooped up my bones and cast them into the sky, where they reformed.

My feet thumped on the floor, and I looked first to my mom, and then to my dad, their faces identical masks of contortion. I realized I was in for a rigorous and unpleasant de-briefing.

Legend holds that a cobra uses its eyes to charm rats before it strikes, but according to Sister Glenda, it is only legend. The fact is, very few creatures are quick enough to escape that reptile's lightning strike, so even a rat's nimblest attempt at escape appears sluggish by comparison. The rat might look beyond the cobra's hood for rescue, or in a final moment of bravado stare its enemy down. It might just as well whip out a banjo to accompany its swan song, because in the end the rat's going to die.

In a moment of clarity I gazed beyond my parents to the four columns, a single stripe hanging from the ceiling along each one. There was a crayon jammed in the pencil sharpener, and in a couple days there would be bits of another mixed among the rabbit droppings. I saw a battered tissue Santa Claus with a gaping wound along one flank, and I knew Santa's toy delivery would be slow that year. For me, Christmas might not come at all. I would be spanked. I would be grounded. I would be sent to Sister Gwendolyn's office, where my flesh would be steamed off my skeleton and turned into sausage.

****

Monday morning oozed in with the same grogginess that accompanies all non-summer Mondays. I popped my pill and wolfed my breakfast, and soon there were no thoughts of fanged Venusians or odiferous ape-bats. Sister Barbara led us through the mysteries of *silent e*, and then she led us into the depths of St. Génevieve's, past the glass-eyed lizards and birds and mammals, both predators and prey. Sister Helga, in a rare flash of silliness, pounded out a jazzy version of "Winter Wonderland" on her piano. As I stared at her monstrous ankles, marveling at how they appeared to overflow her shoes like so much frothy root beer foam, there came a knock at the Dungeon door. We stopped singing just as Mr. Snow Man fell at the hands of his thuggish assailants.

"I need to speak to that one right there!" Sister Beryl announced as she swept into the room.

She was met with a lilting chorus of "Hiiii Sister Beryyyyyl!" from a gaggle of kids who had been to St. Génevière's since kindergarten. I hadn't been, and I wasn't sure what to expect. From the fire in her eyes and the speed with which she covered the distance between the door and my chair, however, I knew not to expect anything pleasant.

"SsssT!" she hissed. "Keep your eyes on Sister Helga!"

But expecting my classmates to return their eyes to Sister Helga would've been like setting them in lawn chairs on the Nebraska prairie and expecting them to concentrate on long division with a tornado blasting through. It was going to be bloody, body parts and chickens would be cast into the stratosphere, and those kids weren't going to miss a bit of it. Not even Valerie Dorazio. Sister Beryl grasped my arm, lifted me out of my chair in the same effortless way Lisa had taken the scissors from her desk drawer, and told Sister Helga to carry on.

The kindergarteners were someplace else when Sister Beryl dragged me into her room, and although there were reading books and fat blue pencils arranged on the tables and a flock of coats along the wall, the room was otherwise just as I had left it the previous Friday evening: a shambles. My intestines slackened to a critical level. For an instant I imagined myself at the mercy of a vexed Venusian fire-hippo, but an uncharacteristic flash of wisdom told me to stay grounded in reality.

"My children came into school this morning expecting to see some pleasant decorations," she said as she glared at me. Her pupils were tiny black pearls of rage. She hauled me over to one of the columns and explained how difficult it had been for her to hang those streamers from the ceiling. She had used a small stepladder and a broomstick, and after twenty minutes of trial and error, she had stumbled upon the proper technique. What had taken her three hours to build, I had demolished in just over thirty minutes.

I was amazed that she didn't ask me *why* I'd wrecked her room. I think, although she didn't excuse it, she seemed to understand it. At least one of us did. As my shame set in, I began to wish she could explain it to me. I knocked down the streamers because I was fascinated by the graceful way they slid off the columns. I've always thought sheep noises were funny, so I terrorized the sheep because it was the only way I could get it to make a sound. But I never *counted the cost* of my behavior, as our minister Reverend Triplett calls it. Everything we enjoy comes at a price, he says, but sometimes other people pay. Like when Curt Ricker knocks Herman Meier's books out of his hands, Curt enjoys it, and Herman pays. I had had a lot of fun Friday afternoon, but Sister Beryl picked up the tab. It was at times like this—after I had broken something precious, hurt someone's feelings, spoken up when I should've piped down—that I always wondered why I did stuff without counting the cost.

I froze in the center of the room when the kindergarteners returned. Sister Beryl kept them on a short leash, and they returned to their deskwork without a peep. They were so well behaved. I was surprised how she ignored me when the class returned. I'd expected her to make an example of me, like she might stick me in a pillory so her kids could throw rotten cabbage at my face. Instead, she allowed me to watch a group of children trying to prepare for the Christmas holidays in a roomful of vandalized decorations. I couldn't even look at Charlie; I was so embarrassed over what his friends must've thought.

Sister Barbara appeared in the doorway and offered to take me off Sister Beryl's hands. Before she dismissed me, Sister Beryl let me know that the decorations would not be replaced that year. There was no need for her to say any more. As Sister Barbara led me on the long, silent walk back to class, I realized that until it became second nature for me to consider

other people's feelings before unleashing my own, I'd continue
to bring moments like this one upon myself.

A Few Words from
Martha McRory and Nina Campbell

Let's get one thing straight right off the bat. We both hate Timothy Larkin. Me and Nina.

Yeah.

Well, maybe *hate* isn't the right word. Sister Ricarda, our Religion teacher, says hating someone means you wish they were dead. So I guess I don't really hate him.

Oh, I hate him.

Shut up! You do not!

I can hate him if I want to.

But once you said you thought he was cute.

Yeah, but I still hate him. Besides, it's his brother who's cute. You just want to squeeze him!

No, Nina. *You* want to squeeze him. He always has a runny nose, like Herman Meier.

Eew! I thought we were talking about Timothy Larkin!

We are! Shut up! Tell me why you hate him.

He's gross.

No, Herman Meier is gross.

Yeah, Martha, but he's the kind of gross that you can't help. Like he was born gross and all the doctor could say was, "Sorry, Mrs. Meier, but your baby was born gross."

What do you think is wrong with him?

Who? Timothy?

Yeah. What's his deal?

Beats me. He's one of those 8OHD kids, I know that. 8O-hyper-destructive, I think it means. Like, 8O on a scale of one to a hundred.

Is that all?

I don't know! He's just gross!

What happened in art class?

I've already told you three times . . . why
weren't you there?

That was right after I got sick. Remember the bus?

Now that was gross! You and Jeff barfed!

Shut up, Nina! I don't want to talk about it!
Anyway . . . art class?

OK, anyways, we're in the art room, right?
Right there across from all those creepy dead
animals. And Sister Natalie has us finger
painting.

Yeah, now *that's* gross. I'm glad I wasn't there.

Oh, I don't know. Finger painting's OK. It
reminds me of when I was a little kid and me
and my sister made mud pies.

You're weird. Anyway, so what happened?

Well, Timothy and Clark are sitting at a table, painting. What do you think about
Clark?

He's OK. Anyway . . .

I think he thinks you're cute.

ANYWAY . . .

One of them catches a spider—

—probably Timothy—

—no, I think it was Clark, actually. Whoever.
So Timothy's dangling it from his hand—
it's making a web, you know, probably trying to get away—and he's pretending like the
spider's a yo-yo. He obviously thought it was
really funny, because then he goes all around
the room showing everybody. "Look!" he keeps
saying. "I have an eight-legged yo-yo!" He
thinks everything he says is funny.

Some of the stuff he says is funny.

Yeah, but he just doesn't know when to stop
being funny, you know?

It's like, everyone else notices when he stops being
funny, and he's always the last person to notice.

Mmm-hmm. Like he runs out of gas, but he's
still rolling.

It's sort of sad.

I told you he was stupid.

No, you said he was gross. Actually, I think he's pretty smart.

>He just doesn't know anything.

No. He doesn't *notice* anything. So what happened with the spider?

>Well, you know I hate bugs. So when Timothy comes over to where I'm sitting, I tell him as nicely as I can, "I don't want to see your stupid spider, Timothy."

But he showed it to you anyway.

>He shows it to me anyway! And when Sister Natalie tells him to sit down and he tries to bring the spider with him, the web gets caught in my hair!

What happened to the spider?

>Well, I could feel the web. It felt like I had a hair falling out, and it got caught on my eyelash—

Gross!

>—so I forgot about the spider, and I forgot I had paint all over my hands—

You didn't!

> —So when I get all that sticky web stuff out of my hair, Cheryl Diorio leans over and says I have paint on my forehead. All because of that stupid Loser Larkin!

I can't believe you forgot you had paint on your fingers! Was it hard to get off your face?

> No, it came right off. But still.

So then what happened?

> So I sit back down to finish my painting— I'm doing a sky, with blue and grey clouds, like a storm's coming?—and there I am making clouds, and I feel this bump in my paint. Sister Natalie showed us how she mixed the paint. You know that powder stuff and water? I'm thinking it's just a hunk of powder that isn't all the way stirred in, so I just keep on . . . fingering, I guess.

But it's the spider, isn't it?

> Right there in the middle of my thunderstorm, and now there's a bunch of spider guts.

What did Sister Natalie say?

Nothing! She didn't know! So I turn around and look at Timothy and I tell him I hate him, but I don't really say it—

You just mouth it, right?

Yeah. But he can't read lips 'cause he's stupid, so he comes over and says "What?" And I show him the spider guts and I'm all ready to throw up, and he sticks his finger into the spider guts and says all I need to do is move it around in the paint and it'll disappear, but he's got orange paint on his fingers, and now I've got an orange streak in the middle of my painting!

So it looked like a sunset. So what?

Whose side are you on, Martha? If I wanted to paint a sunset, I would've painted a sunset!

I just don't think it's that big a deal.

That's because you've never had a spider web stuck in your hair.

Yes, I have.

When?!

Remember when we went to Andrew's farm? I think you were riding the horse—with Timothy!

Don't remind me . . .

I think a piece of one was floating in the air—

Like in *Charlotte's Web*?

Oh, that was the saddest story, wasn't it?

You feel so bad for the pig—what's his name?

Wilbur, right?

I think so.

Do you think Timothy feels like that?

What—like a pig?

Well, you know how mad people get at him sometimes.

Yeah, so?

Well, do you think he feels like Wilbur did when all the spiders flew away?

Are you kidding?

No! I mean, he has to know how people feel about him, right?

Probably not right away. He keeps rolling. Remember?

But he has to figure it out after a while, right?

I guess so.

So, do you see what I mean?

Who cares? He stuck a spider in my face!

Yeah, but do you really think he came over to you meaning to stick a spider in your face?

Who knows?

I didn't ask you if you knew. I asked you if you thought.

No. I guess he didn't.

So it was an accident?

Maybe.

Do you think that's why he has to take those pills? Those 8OHD pills?

What do you mean?

You know, like because he has accidents and he doesn't always know when he isn't being funny anymore?

> But who wants to have to take a pill every day?

Nobody. Timothy probably doesn't want to either. Do you think he'd like it if he knew we were talking about him?

> Everybody talks about him. There's something wrong with someone who has to take a pill every day.

My mom has to take a pill every day.

> Is she hyper, too?

Yeah, but it's another kind of hyper. Hypertentious or whatever. Something about her blood pressure, I think. Like she could be sitting there watching TV and all of a sudden get really mad—like at my little brother?—and all her veins could just blow up.

> Eew!

But it's not her fault, is what I'm trying to say.

> So you're saying the stuff Timothy does isn't his fault either?

Oh, I didn't say that, but maybe it's not his fault that he doesn't notice when he's not being funny anymore.

> I think he knows exactly what he's doing. He stuck a spider in my hair.

I thought that was an accident. Have you ever seen him try to hurt somebody on purpose?

> He makes fun of your hair.

So do you!

> But I'm allowed, 'cause we're friends.

I still don't like it.

> Well, soooorry!

And I don't think he's gross, either.

> I knew it! You like him!

Well, I don't hate him. What about you?

> He's OK, I guess. But I still hate him.

B

"Holy Crow, a magic show!" I heard Clark shout to nobody in particular as I was hanging my coat on my peg. I jammed my hat and mittens into my cubby and ran into the room.

"Where? *Really*?" I must've shouted. Across the room, Clark and Nina and Martha were too wrapped up in the details to look at me, so I ran over to them and shouted again.

The girls just rolled their eyes, but Clark filled me in. "It's 'cause it's February, and always in February they have a show, and this time it's gonna be a *magic* show!"

"An *illusion* show," Nina and Martha corrected him.

"What's an illusion show?" I asked. I'd never heard that word before. To me it sounded like a slideshow of somebody's vacation to an Alaskan island. Clark was all out of breath. Whatever this was, it was going to be good.

"It's when somebody comes out and does tricks and stuff," he continued.

"Magic," I said.

Nina and Martha rolled their eyes again. "You're so stupid, Timothy," Nina said. "It's not *real* magic, 'cause real magic doesn't exist. Besides, nuns aren't supposed to do magic. It's like a vowel or something."

I turned to Clark. "We're going to see a *nun* magician?"

Nina and Martha huffed at me and walked off. Before Clark could answer, Sister Barbara marched into the room. By February we knew to take our seats before she said a word. In fact, normally we would've been in trouble for not being seated already, but I could tell even Sister Barbara was excited.

"Sister?" I asked, forgetting to raise my hand. "Are we going to see a nun magician?"

"A couple people who have forgotten the classroom rules might miss out," she replied without looking at me, correcting me without encouraging my behavioral gaffe.

So it was true! Sister Barbara said the show would take place in the auditorium right after lunch. Clark and I looked at each other like it was suddenly Christmas, and Nina and Martha rolled their eyes again. I sat up straight in my chair and folded my hands like a good boy. I didn't know who was going to miss out on the show, but I wanted to make sure it wouldn't be me. I conducted myself like a gentleman, and when Andrew Hockenberry had the hiccups during the Pledge, I hardly laughed at all.

But later I had problems.

There's an old amusement park cut out of the forest about a half-hour down the road from St. Géneviève's. It started out as a merri-go-round almost a century ago. There's a storybook section full of Mother Goose characters for kids who are too small for any of the rides. Across from that are little rides for kids like Charlie, who don't wear diapers anymore but still poop sometimes when they shouldn't. Then over the years they've added bigger, fancier rides that go fast enough to make you throw up your funnel cake. Around all of that is a miniature train track, where you can ride in red and yellow passenger cars pulled by a genuine steam locomotive. It carries people across a small river and over to a petting zoo, then it winds through the woods for close to a mile before rolling back into the station.

My mom really likes the train, but I think it's boring because it doesn't go fast, and I don't believe it's ever made anyone throw up. But if you think it goes slow on the way to the petting zoo, just wait until it crosses the river on its way back to the station. Trains aren't like ice skates, where you can stop anytime you want to just by slamming into the wall. Trains take forever to stop. Some actually have to start slow-ing down before they even get going. That's what my dad says anyway. That's what the rest of my morning felt like. Like a fully loaded train, the day started off slow, and then it got slower and slower, waiting for that magic show.

(*Illusion* show.)

All I could think of for the rest of the morning was how great it would be if I could do magic. If Nina or Martha ever said something dumb, I could wave my fingers at them and turn them into guppies. I could turn my books into a rabid badger, and when Curt Ricker tried to slap them out of my hands, it would bite his fingers off. Of course, then I'd probably get in trouble, so I'd need to be able to zap everything back to normal afterward. Not that Nina and Martha are normal.

I could snap my fingers and fly over the lawn and throw pinecones at the girls playing hopscotch. And because I could fly, they'd be too impressed to yell at me. Oh, and I'd whip Clark in all our dogfights, because he'd never be able to get off the runway! For him it'd be like trying to engage enemy fighter planes with a station wagon.

Of course, I could probably make him fly, too. We could fly over the rooftops of the school and those girls wouldn't matter at all anymore. I'd just have to find out how easy it would be to fly and make someone else fly at the same time. I've read that it takes concentration to cast a spell, and people don't usually associate me with concentration. I will say I'm pretty good at that game where you lay a deck of cards facedown and then try to match them up: I just can't remember what the game's called.

About the time I felt like I should have a long, white, Rip Van Winkle beard, Sister Barbara dismissed us for lunch. We snaked single file up the hall, down the Grand Staircase, did an about-face in the foyer, and descended a half-level to the auditorium. I peeked in through the double doors as we marched by. A couple hundred folding chairs were lined up facing the stage, and on the stage stood a small magician's table, sort of a narrow crate standing on its end. I couldn't get a good look at it without stopping the line behind me (I had a sudden vision of my problems with the devil doorknob at Hockenberry Farm), but it appeared to be bright purple with clouds painted on it. I couldn't wait! A nun magician!

I sat in the cafeteria and pushed a slab of rainbow beef around on my plate for another couple years. (When the light hits the beef a certain way, you can see a rainbow in it. Probably bacteria.) The train was taking forever, and the station seemed to be getting farther and farther away. Two big secondary girls were in the cafeteria at the same time we were, and instead of sitting at a table by themselves, they decided to sit with Clark and me. They laughed and talked about things that I couldn't understand, mostly about the boys in their classes. I figured out that much, anyway. What I couldn't understand was how it sounded like they almost *liked* those boys. Now, I've always liked Valerie Dorazio, but have you ever heard me talk about her? No, you have not. To me, there are certain things you don't admit. Boys don't talk about liking girls, girls don't talk about liking boys, and only boys can talk about peeing.

But then they started talking about the nun magic show. "I just love Sister Hish," one of them said. "She came to our church once."

"Wait a minute, wait a minute," Clark interrupted. "Sister *Hish*?"

"Uh-huh," the other one said. "Sister Hishafeffaweffenheffer. She's Dutch or something."

Clark and I looked at the girls as if they'd just traded heads.

"Hishafeffaweffenheffer," she repeated. "Actually, a classic example of throchaic tetrameter."

"Indeed. Classic," the first girl agreed—the one with the fat nose. I could actually see right up her nose. All the way to Vermont, my Uncle George would've said. She could've had cats living up there.

"Eight syllables," the other one said. "With accents on the odd syllables. Like MIST a FED a DEAF-en ZEPH-yr. HISHaFEFfaWEFfenHEFfer!"

"Trochaic tetrameter!"

Those girls were so smart. I had no idea what kind of stuff you learn in high school, but I was beginning to believe those folks up there had a name for everything. Like if your mom cooks meatloaf at home and she pays real close attention to the recipe, but still you find this grey skin-looking thing stuck in among the meat bits that not even she can identify; well there's probably a name for it, and I'll bet you that's what you learn in high school.

Suddenly I was glad they were there. I tried picking their brains about everything we were going to see at the show. Unfortunately, the girls thought it would be funny to tell us just enough about Sister (Hish?) to get us really worked up.

"I don't know," said the one with the nose. "She's probably changed her show since last year, when that kid died."

Clark and I nearly sprang out of our seats. "What kid?!" I demanded. I'll admit now, I wasn't very savvy as a first grader.

"I think it was during the levitation trick, wasn't it?" the other girl asked. "Didn't he just float off into space?"

"No, that kid just got caught up in the lights. They had to send up his meals with a pulley," said the one with the nose. "No, this kid, the one who died, was sitting in the audience. It was the trick with the duck."

"Oh, yeah, that's right," the other girl said, bowing her head and crossing herself. A hush fell over the table. The girl with the nose knew Clark and I wanted to know what had happened, but by this time we were too overwhelmed to speak in complete sentences.

"See," she continued in a quiet tone, "normally the way the trick works is that Sister Hish fires a duck out of a cannon. Boom!" she shouted, and slammed her hands on the table loud enough to make us jump. I think even the other girl jumped. I started having second thoughts about Sister Hisha-whatten-ever. "She holds up what looks like a tennis ball can, there's a flash of orange fire, and this duck flies out of the can and out over the audience."

"Might be a pigeon," the other girl corrected.

"Might be. But last year they were serving this same roast beef, and Sister Hishafeffaweffenheffer went back for seconds, and then she had thirds."

The other girl nodded and picked up the story. "So her magical powers were just bursting at the seams, and when she called for the pigeon—"

"I still think it was a duck . . ."

"This huge raven flew out instead—"

"I think it was a vulture. Black one . . ."

"And instead of soaring over the audience and out the door, it shot straight into the fourth row and stuck some kid in the throat like a huge, wing-flappy spear."

"Right in the throat!" the Nose repeated, and for emphasis poked me in the throat with her finger. "Beak popped out the other side, like a stick through a marshmallow." Then she composed herself and shook her head. "Kid was dead before they could even call his mom."

"Sad," the other one whispered. "I heard they had to bury him in an extra large coffin because they couldn't remove the bird."

"That's right. They just folded it over his chest and pulled the covers up under his chin. People who went to the funeral said he looked just like he'd fallen asleep with a big black bird on his chest."

We paused to allow this to settle in, and then Clark broke the silence. "Didn't they put her in jail?"

"Oh, you can't put a magician in jail," the Nose said, sweeping her hand through space, adding to her air of authority. "Especially Sister Hish. She'd walk right out."

"Just like you can't keep acid in a bottle," the other one said, "because it'll eat through the bottom. Then through the floor. If you spill enough you're gonna have a bunch of upset Chinese people with burns on their feet." I hadn't considered any of these things. It couldn't believe how much these girls knew. "Besides," she said, "Sister Hish didn't kill the kid. The bird did. And he was just a first grader anyway."

The Nose nodded in agreement. "I heard his parents just started over with a new kid, and he got the old kid's room and all his stuff. And he's much better behaved."

I looked at Clark and he looked at me. I didn't want to go to the magic show anymore. Right there in my seat in front of the girl with the nose and her smaller-nosed friend, I begged God to stop the train. Maybe throw it in reverse. My prayers were shattered when Sister Barbara rang her hand bell, signaling the end of lunch.

A storm surge of students flooded the landing of the Black Staircase and rushed toward the auditorium. I felt like a salmon pushed upstream by his brothers and sisters, all of whom wanted to find husbands and wives and weren't afraid of catching cooties. I guess I wasn't afraid of cooties either—in matters of Valerie Dorazio, for instance, they might not even exist—but I had a feeling there were grizzly bears lurking in the headwaters.

The first thing you learn at assembly is that orders can come from all sorts of grownups you've never spoken to before. "Button that lip, young man!" "Hands to yourself!" "Single file!" "Sit there!" "No, right THERE!" So it was that I found myself sitting at the end of a row of second graders, with Clark nowhere in sight. I tried to warn the kid next to me about the lethal raven, but he just gave me an ugly look. Then I realized that, being a second grader, he already knew all about it. In fact, the more I thought about it, I realized that he and the dead kid must've been friends.

I leaned over to him and whispered, "I'm really sorry for your loss."

Just then the house lights went down, and the stage glowed under white and yellow spots. I wanted to ask the kid next to me where the levitated boy had ended up, but I decided against it for fear of stirring up more bad memories.

"Good afternoon, students," boomed a familiar and very businesslike voice. It was Sister Gwendolyn, addressing the audience as she crossed to center stage. I could see the purple table trying to creep away from her. "It is with great pleasure that I welcome back to St. Génévieve's Academy a very dear friend of mine, Sister Hishafeffaweffenheffer. Sister?"

As applause welled up from all over the auditorium, a cannonball-shaped figure rolled out from the curtains on the right. An arm appeared from the circular mass, and a hand waved. A gunfight of thoughts fired through my head as the figure approached Sister Gwendolyn at center stage. *Of course!* I reasoned, *It's only natural that Sister Gwendolyn should be friends with someone who uses magic to slay unsuspecting kids by shooting large birds at them! They probably share a cauldron and everything!*

Sister Gwendolyn shook Sister Hishafeffaweffenheffer's hand and exited.

"Hello children!" Sister Hishafeffaweffenheffer shouted, her round face opening into a huge smile like a split cantaloupe. She waved again with her other hand as the student body returned her greeting. She said a few things about how she hoped we were all studying hard and making our parents happy, but I was too busy keeping an eye out for that large-bore tennis ball can to register everything she said. Somehow she was suddenly holding a huge yellow umbrella and there were tiny finches flapping around her head. I was relieved, judging by the size of those birds, that she hadn't taken the lion's share of rainbow beef, but I was alarmed by the lightning-quick appearance of the umbrella. I'll bet that poor kid last year didn't have a chance to flinch.

Sister Hishafeffaweffenheffer didn't look like a regular nun. She wore a veil, sort of like the other sisters, but it wasn't black or grey. Instead, it was the same purple as the magician's table, which was the same purple as the robe she wore. I also noticed that there were little yellow birds flying among the clouds on the table and the robe. I couldn't see her feet at all, but I wouldn't have been surprised to find she didn't have any.

The finches flew offstage in the same direction Sister Gwendolyn had gone. I figured by the next trick Sister Gwendolyn would be finishing lunch and picking the feathers out of her teeth with a fountain pen. Sister Hishafeffaweffenheffer explained what illusions are as she performed tricks involving metal rings, a rabbit in a box, milk that disappeared into a newspaper and flowers that sprang out of it, and a few things with fire. But it all sure looked like magic to me.

She produced a bronze dish and laid it on the table. Then she wadded up the flowers she'd pulled out of the newspaper and stuffed them into the dish. She waved her hands over the dish and the flowers burst into flames. Big clouds of smoke burped out of the dish as she covered it with a lid. When the smoke died down, she removed the lid and a white pigeon jumped out of the dish and into her hands. Like my friend Herman says, sometimes fire really does change things. The audience roared with approval, but I became even more anxious because the woman simply would not stop making birds. And they seemed to be getting bigger.

Sister Hishafeffaweffenheffer rolled her hands over each other and the pigeon disappeared. Then she reached behind the table and held up a white metal tube about a foot long—just big enough to hold a few tennis balls! She flipped it backwards in her hand the way a gunslinger twirls a six-shooter, and then she pointed it over the audience.

I sometimes have dreams where I'm running from something big and scary—maybe an ogre or a hungry pterodactyl—and each time it feels like my feet are stuck in swamp muck. The harder I run, the slower I go. This was not the case that afternoon as I bolted toward the auditorium door. It took my shadow a few seconds to notice I was gone. I made it to the hall, heard a loud *bang!* and covered my head.

The *bang!* turned out to be the auditorium door slamming behind me. I spun and peeked through the window, and what I saw turned my guts to jelly. It was horrifying, and I still have the image burned onto my retinas to this very day. There stood Sister Gwendolyn, staring at me through the glass. I stood frozen in the way mice aren't really supposed to be hypnotized by snakes, and then she stepped through the door. I don't even remember the door opening. I think she actually stepped *through* it, like a malevolent vapor.

"Come with me, young man," she whispered, and I could smell coffee on her breath. It sort of reminded me of my dad, to be honest, the way I sometimes smell coffee when he helps me with my homework after supper. Then I worried that maybe she'd eaten my dad. She escorted me up the east wing corridor, past Sister Carrie's clinic, to a room I'd never seen before.

Afternoon sunlight filtered through open blinds and across two living room chairs and a desk. The desk was neat, but covered with stacks of books, manila folders, and a portrait of three red-haired girls. Sister Gwendolyn guided me to one of the chairs and handed me a tissue. Up to that point I didn't even realize I'd been crying. "Wait right here," she said.

"Y-y-yes, Ma'am." It was one of the first times I ever remember stuttering.

A miniature grandfather clock ticked away on a bookshelf as I looked around the room. Behind the desk was a large picture of a snow-covered field. In the distance were mountains, and beyond them was blue sky. A lonely buffalo with snow in his fur was grazing in the foreground. Apart from the sliver of sky, the picture was mostly black-and-white, even though I could tell it was in color.

In one corner of the room was a small table made of dark wood, the fancy kind Grandma Larkin has next to her bed.

But instead of an alarm clock and a glass with teeth in it, there was a violin propped up on a thin metal stand. From someplace else in the room, I couldn't tell where, I could hear soft classical music.

I wasn't sure where I was, but it was clear whoever kept this office liked very pretty things. I sat and listened to the music. It was bouncy and familiar; my parents would know the title. Some of their music was boring, but I had to admit, some of it could really change my mood. Like that song about the river that runs through Prague, or the one about that big gate in Russia. The music coming from the hidden radio almost made me forget I was sitting in that office, waiting for Sister Gwendolyn to return and drag me to *her* office. The room made me think about being home on a Sunday afternoon.

I continued to scan the office, fascinated by everything I saw. There was a wooden crucifix on the wall beside the window, just like every other room at St. Géneviève's. Then one thing caught my eye that I hadn't noticed before. On the far corner of the desk, mostly hidden behind the black rotary phone, was a little plastic Snoopy sitting on his doghouse! He was wearing his flying ace goggles and a wicked sneer. There was a tiny hole just behind him along the roofline. An electric pencil sharpener?

Where was I?

I thought of Snoopy doing his beagle dance, arms outstretched, head thrown back, feet a blur. The music helped. The tempo was bright and spirited. It was so familiar. I thought of Santa Claus bouncing through the snow on a Christmas morning, eating candy and laughing as all the children played with their new toys. Maybe Paul Bunyan, laughing and chopping down trees the way you'd kick over a dandelion. That music . . .

The song was about Jupiter, although Sister Helga down in the Dungeon would say that it's not a *song*, it's a *piece*. Like a *piece* of pie. I suddenly realized why she was so big.

Not Jupiter the planet, but Jupiter the Roman god of happiness. By the time I recognized it, the piece was over. Saturn should be next, the god of old age, I think. I wondered why old age would follow happiness, like two separate parts of a train. First you're happy, but then you get old. My grandparents always seemed happy though, as if they'd gotten the plan mixed up.

I thought about my grandparents. They had lots of wrinkles, but according to pictures I'd seen, they didn't have so many when they were my parents' age. They almost looked like different people, but you could tell they weren't. And somehow, they looked the same. Then I wondered how many wrinkles they'd have by the time I'd grown up. My dad once told me you get a new brain wrinkle every time you learn something new. He said he's learned so much, his brain's all smooth again. Maybe when I'm grown up my grandparents will be as smooth as they were when they were younger.

Saturn, the god of old age. Sister Gwendolyn had a lot of wrinkles, and she didn't seem very happy. Maybe she knew something my grandparents didn't. It didn't occur to me that it might be vice versa.

The piece ended quietly, the way a planet would vanish in the rear view mirror of a speeding spaceship. Next stop, Uranus!

Oh no! Uranus, the magician!

Almost on cue, Sister Gwendolyn swept back into the room, and (speak of the devil) who should be behind her in proper planetary order but Sister Hishafeffaweffenheffer herself?

I didn't know who to watch. I felt like a stray elk, separated from the herd by a pair of ravenous wolves.

I missed you with my bird the first time, little boy, I could almost hear Sister Hishafeffaweffenheffer say, *so I came back for another shot!*

"All right, then, Mr. Larkin?" Sister Gwendolyn asked as she sat behind the desk.

I nodded. For a moment Sister Gwendolyn was at bay; at least she was outside of arm's reach. I turned my eyes on Sister Hishafeffaweffenheffer, who settled into the chair beside me. She was no longer wearing her purple robe with the clouds and birds on the front. She looked more natural in a black habit similar to the ones the other sisters wore. She really looked like Sister Helga, but she smiled a lot more.

"I'm sorry if I frightened you, young man," she said, and then she leaned closer like she wanted to tell me a secret. "I really just wanted to make you laugh." I suddenly liked her. "It's not really magic, you know. I'm just like you," she said. Then turning to Sister Gwendolyn, she added with a laugh, "I'm just a whole lot heavier!"

"Then how do you do all those tricks? And what about the dead kid?" I asked.

Sister Hishafeffaweffenheffer again turned to Sister Gwendolyn, this time with a puzzled look on her face.

Sister Gwendolyn closed her eyes and shook her head the same way my mom and Sister Barbara do so often when I'm around and said, "There's no telling."

Sister Hishafeffaweffenheffer looked back at me and told me about the art of misdirection. "It's also called sleight-of-hand. I grab your attention with one hand, and you forget to notice what the other hand is doing." She opened her hands, crossed them, waved one, and then pulled a raspberry out of my ear with the other. "Misdirection!" she repeated, eating the raspberry.

I trembled again at the notion of the way wolves hunt.

"It gives her the *illusion* of magical abilities," Sister Gwendolyn explained.

"And that's it?" I asked.

"That," replied Sister Hishafeffaweffenheffer, "and lots of practice in front of the mirror. That's the hardest part, really."

"Why's that?"

She laughed like Jupiter and asked, "Would you want to spend hours in front of a mirror if you had a face like this?"

I liked her, but I was still too afraid to laugh.

"One of the things I tell my students is that misdirection happens all the time in life," she said. "We pay lots of attention to the things we like—playing, for example—and sometimes we forget to notice the things we need—such as listening to our parents."

I asked her if playing was bad, because a lot of the sisters at the school seemed to think so, and she laughed again. "Oh heavens, no! In fact, sometimes people *need* to play! Sister Gwendolyn plays her violin over there! But sometimes we need to pay attention to things that are more important, even if they aren't the most—"

Everything else she said was lost when I realized I was sitting in Sister Gwendolyn's office! Where were the meat hooks? Where was the trapdoor? And what was Snoopy doing here? The world was suddenly a far different place than the one I'd awakened to that morning. In one sense I was more at peace because a few things were suddenly less threatening, more normal. But I couldn't help feeling a bit disappointed because a few things were suddenly less exciting, more normal.

"Sister?" I interrupted. "Is your name really Hishafeffaweffenheffer?"

She smiled again and shook her head. "No, child. That's all for fun."

"What's your real name?" I glanced over at Sister Gwendolyn. "May I ask?"

Sister Hishafeffaweffenheffer smiled. "Bea."

I stared at her. "B?"

"Beatrice, actually. But I'll answer to Bea. Or just B."

I suddenly wanted her as my third grandma. And even though she still scared me, for a few minutes I might've taken Sister Gwendolyn as my aunt.

"Sister B?" I asked, "Do you know where they keep acid so it won't leak out everywhere?"

Sister B looked back at Sister Gwendolyn, who again closed her eyes and shook her head in that familiar way.

Kickball at St. Géneviève's

My mom took me to the mall once to get clothes for Easter. I've never liked Easter clothes because they don't look like normal clothes. They're always blue like the sky or yellow like scrambled eggs. They make you look too much like *you* belong in an Easter basket, nestled into that stringy fake grass, side-by-side and cheek-to-cheek with a bunch of those yellow baby marshmallow chickens. I don't really like those baby chickens either. I have a tough time calling them candy because they're not chocolate. And unless you're talking about those pink after-dinner mints that taste sort of buttery and turn into minty little snowflakes in your mouth, candy that isn't chocolate is like a religious person who doesn't believe in God.

Once there was a Greek guy named Achilles, who lived a long, long time ago. He was a mighty soldier who swung a mighty sword and cut off lots of people's heads. Achilles received invincibility when his doctor grabbed him by the ankle and dipped him into the River Styx. (I've read that the River Styx runs through *Aitch-Ee-Double-Hockey-Sticks*, but my dad swears it runs through Cleveland, Ohio, and it caught fire one day in 1969. I'm not sure what that says about Cleveland.) Whenever you'd tried to cut off Achilles' head, it was like trying to whack the head off a statue. *Clank!* Then you'd flash an embarrassed grin, apologize, and then wait for Achilles to bop you one. Arrows bounced off of him like sparrows off a picture window, and he probably would've been the first kid picked for every kickball game in the world if he'd been alive when kickball was invented.

He might've had his chance, but he had a problem with his ankle, the one the doctor held when he dipped him. That was the one place where Achilles could be injured, and don't you know an arrow nicked him on that very ankle? The fact is, if Achilles had taken just a couple minutes to rinse the cut and dab on a little monkey blood, he might've been OK. But he was too busy cutting off people's heads, and he got a nasty infection and died. That's why, when we dip our dog for fleas, we make sure not to hold him by the ankles.

My whole point about Achilles is that before the people who make those yellow baby chickens box them up and sell them to people like my mom, I'll bet they dip them in the River Styx. Every year I get three or four of them in my Easter basket, and every year I try one. As always, I ram the whole thing in my mouth and bite down on it, and I can feel it goosh out between my molars like florescent yellow sausage.

I'm sure it's like that with everyone.

What most folks haven't considered, though, is that if not for your saliva melting that little baby chicken into yellow drool, you could open your mouth and spit it back out, and in about a minute it would spring back to its original shape, looking every bit as chicken-ish as it had before you got the bright idea to eat it. Achilles had nothing on those yellow baby chickens.

At this point Sister Barbara might roll her eyes and ask me what Achilles and those yellow baby chickens have to do with shopping for Easter clothing. Well, simply this:

I really don't like Easter clothes. That's not to say I don't like dressing up. I'm used to that. St. Géneviève's had a dress code. When I first heard about it, I thought *dress code* meant spies patrolling the halls in evening gowns, whispering to each other in muted tones about how the *roosters in Reykjavik rarely dance after sundown*. But it really just meant there were rules about what students could wear. The girls could wear anything they wanted to, as long as it was the same green plaid skirt and white oxford blouse that all the other girls wore. It was much better being a boy, because we could wear all sorts of different colors, as long as we wore slacks (Great-granddad

Larkin calls them *Sunday-go-to-meetin' pants*), a button-down shirt, and a tie. I found out later that most kids would throw up if they had to wear a tie to school, but I liked it because it didn't feel like I was going to school at all—at least not until I got there and had to sit by Cheryl Diorio and her spitty finger tips. It felt like I was going to work, just like my dad.

But Easter clothes aren't good for any other date on the calendar but Easter. Unfortunately, my mom doesn't see it that way. The day after Easter in first grade, I had to wear my Easter suit to school (Mom made me march straight to my room and hang it up the moment we got home from church, so it was still pretty clean). For once I didn't feel like I was going to work, because in all the times I've watched my dad back out of the driveway on his way to the office, he's never once looked like he should be nestled in a pile of fake grass next to one of those sticky yellow baby chickens.

At recess I didn't feel like a fighter plane buzzing the loathsome Hopscotch Battalion of the Third Reich; I felt like a drippy little kid dressed as a blue Easter egg, running with his arms outstretched, just *pretending* to be a fighter plane buzzing the loathsome Hopscotch Battalion of the Third Reich. I think any drama coach worth his pay will tell you that if you can't sell the role to yourself, you'll never sell it to your audience. That day the girls' aims were truer, their insults more acute, and I felt their flak more keenly than I ever had before. And I knew that since they had found my own Achilles heel, their attacks would be just as vicious from then on, even on the days when I flew low over their base clad in brown corduroys, a raging inferno in my eye. I had no other ammunition in my arsenal. Water pistols were forbidden at St. Géneviève's, and I wouldn't learn how to launch pasty, deep-throated snot loogies until after I started public school.

On Mondays we had gym class right after lunch. That particular Monday was sunny and unseasonably warm for early spring, and Mr. Unger decided to take us out on the back lawn for kickball. The back lawn at St. Géneviève's was one of the most peaceful places anywhere. Technically, it's no longer the *back* lawn, any more than the space where Clark and I used to fly our Corsairs is the front lawn. Now it's all simply a grassy lot surrounded by ancient oak trees. But on that day we strolled single file through a back door beyond the cafeteria and into a lush meadow that rolled gently uphill away from the school. The emerald aroma of cut grass greeted us as we gathered in the center of the meadow to hear Mr. Unger's instructions. Catbirds and orioles sang in the trees off to each side, and I was quickly distracted by my surroundings. I had a pretty good grip on the subtleties of kickball anyway, so I passed the time surveying this uncharted region.

The trees on either side of the meadow reached toward each other like a great, green horseshoe, leaving a narrow gap in the center. This opening led to an old cemetery, speckled with scores of dazzling white grave markers. The markers were all roughly the same size, and they were all simple rectangles and crosses. Mr. Unger told us that priests and sisters from as far back as the 1800's were buried up there, many of whom had taught at St. Géneviève's at one time or another.

Mr. Unger wasn't one of the sisters at St. Géneviève's. He wasn't even a priest. I'm not sure how he ended up teaching there, but because of who he was and what we did in his class, I always figured his first name was Gym. He had a great way of teaming us up for kickball. He'd pick two captains (I was never a captain), and the first captain always picked the biggest kid—Richard Irwin. But then the second captain got to pick the next two kids. Everybody except the girls and me and Herman Meier would yell, "Pick me! Pick me!" I think we knew better. The second captain, unless he was David DeFloria, would pick David DeFloria and Clark. If he *was* David DeFloria, he'd pick Clark and somebody else. But if both Richard and David were captains (which never happened, but it could've), the first captain would've picked Clark, and the other captain would've picked two other kids, neither of whom would've been Herman Meier or me.

After that, Mr. Unger would tell the first captain to pick a couple girls, then the second captain would pick two. Now here's what I liked: Mr. Unger would then tell the first captain to pick a little guy. It didn't matter who got picked, me or Herman, neither of us got picked last. It wasn't like recess, where the kids were in charge. Mr. Unger always arranged it so some mid-sized boy got picked last, and it was never the same boy. Mr. Unger was pretty big—bigger than my dad, even—but I think he must've been a little guy when he was a kid, because he knew about people like me.

Good old Gym Unger.

Clark was a captain that day, and I was on his team. Nina and Martha were on Book (rhymes with Spook—beats me why) Dovenspike's team, so I knew we were going to have fun. I had planned to make it my business to step on their feet as I rounded the bases, but Book-rhymes-with-Spook stuck them in the outfield, where I could still hear them giggling about my Easter pants. Valerie Dorazio was notably absent. That was kind of disappointing, but I was able to play better without having to worry about messing up in front of her.

We were up first. Andrew Hockenberry kicked the first pitch of the game straight over second base, and it didn't stop rolling until Book-rhymes-with-Spook yelled for Martha and Nina to go get it. By that time, Andrew had run all the way around the bases and had fallen headlong into the grass fifteen feet from home. "Water!" he gasped, clutching his throat and crawling toward home. "I'm dying! I need water!" Mr. Unger told him to get up, which he did. The run counted, but Andrew was called out because of unsportsmanlike conduct. We still thought it was pretty funny.

Cheryl Diorio was up next (Mr. Unger made us kick boy-girl-boy-girl), and she didn't like the look of the pitch when it rolled her way. She bent over and stopped it, and Book-rhymes-with-Spook yelled at her. I don't think he was worried about her cheating—she couldn't kick the ball very far anyway—I just think he didn't want slobber on the ball. Cheryl took a step back, addressed the ball (meaning she stared at it like she hated it—*I really* hate *that ball* . . .), lunged forward, and kicked the air next to it. The ball eased itself to the left in the draft of her foot, and she waddled off lickety-split toward third base.

"Safe!" Mr. Unger shouted.

The other team said it wasn't fair, but Mr. Unger was laughing too hard to call her out. He did, in all fairness and sportsmanship, make her cross over to first base.

I was up next, and I booted a screamer down the third base line. For a moment I forgot I looked like an Easter egg, and I tore up the first base line. Smoke streamed from my loafers, and I'm sure I left curls in the air, just like in the cartoons when somebody runs really fast. I had no idea if anyone had caught the ball, but I knew I could make it to second base, if only—

"Run, you little puke!" I shouted at Cheryl Diorio, who was firmly planted in the baseline between first and second. It probably wasn't a nice thing to say, but there she was, standing a few steps off first, her back to the play, shouting something about her shoes to Nina and Martha out in right field. I roared past her, hoping some of my speed curls would get tangled in her hair.

Second base came into view like the deck of an aircraft carrier. I didn't know if the ball was on its way or not, but I was coming in for an emergency landing. I extended my wingtips and lowered my gear. If the tail hook didn't catch, I knew I'd be a goner. Wisps of low-level clouds blurred past my canopy as I drew a bead on the leading edge of the carrier runway. I squinted against the rays of the Pacific sun, pulled back on the throttle, and came down hard on the unyielding deck. A bullet of pain shot up my left thigh as my landing gear collapsed with a deafening RIP!

In the stupor caused by my abrupt landing, I slumped over my controls, oblivious to the raging flames consuming the fuselage. I would have succumbed to the smoke had I not been roused by shouting just outside my canopy:

"Major Larkin!" the voice pleaded. "Larkin! Snap out of it, man!"

Hey, Idiot! You tore your pants!

"Huh?" I muttered, choking in the dissipating smoke.

And you're out, you bonehead! You passed a runner on the base path!

I stared down the length of my body, covered in dust and clad not in a dashing flight suit, but in unappetizing polyester robin-shell blue. My bruised and bloody leg peeked out from a jagged tear in the material above my left knee. The impact should've broken my hip, but somehow I'd been spared. I stood up and dusted myself off. As I did, I noticed a lump in my left pocket I couldn't account for. I pulled the pocket inside out, and there it was—smeared across my palm, its white guts glistening in the sun. It was one of those yellow baby chickens, a victim of the one thing on this Earth more potent than itself—that violent sport of flying aces and kings, Kickball at St. Géneviève's.

That afternoon I made a vow over its battered corpse to digest with great ceremony one of its kin when I got home—a solemn tribute to the one who gave its life for the good of the squadron.

. . . But Never Pink

Sister Glenda had a rule about the bathroom. If you needed
to go, you had to write your name on the chalkboard first.
We didn't use hall passes. Before anyone heard the story of
Sister Helga's Class and the Glass Animal Boxes, as it came to
be called, students were trusted to get where they were supposed to be without goofing off. And the way the boys' room
reeked, people didn't spend any more time in there than they
had to.

Sister Glenda taught science, one of my favorite classes. My dad enjoyed science in school, and it was understood
that I should grow up to enjoy it, too. He liked space in particular, and to this day we'll take walks at night and he'll point
out constellations and planets to anyone who will listen.
"Boys, that cluster of stars over there is called the Pleiades, or
the Seven Sisters. That bright star below Orion is Sirius, the
Dog Star," he'll tell us. "And boys, if you look just over the
treetops in the Michwiczs' front yard, you'll see Castor and
Pollux." Charlie and I always look, but all we ever see are
stars.

I like the sky and the stars, but when my dad starts talking about them, he gets excited like they're handing out Wonka
bars and he's first in line. "Boys, there's the Milky Way, and if
you look real fast, the Big Dipper is handing out gum!" I like
science for all the gross stuff. My folks bought me a micro-
scope and some slides for my birthday, and my favorite slide
was a squashed fly. It was all hairy and dyed purple, and at
40x, it looked like something the plumber once fished out of
our bathtub drain. Gross, but the kind of gross I really like. I
brought it in and showed Sister Glenda, and she liked it, too.
That's why I think it's good that the grossest thing that ever

happened to me at St. Génevière's happened in Sister Glenda's class.

It all began with breakfast. My mom will tell you my worst habit is that I don't move very fast in the morning, especially in winter. Back then we had a big bathroom with soft carpet and a heater right next to the tub. Once I got moving it never took me very long to get out of my pajamas and into my school clothes, but I'd spend an hour curled up in a ball next to the heater. Mom called it *roosting*—like, "You can get dressed in the bathroom, but don't go in there and *roost*!" Still, I became quite an accomplished rooster. The trade-off, unfortunately, was that I never had time for a decent breakfast. So instead of cereal or even breakfast pastries, my mom bought me some of that breakfast-in-an-envelope stuff, sort of like what astronauts eat. You just dump it in a glass of milk, stir it, drink it, burp, wipe your mouth on your sleeve, then go and brush your teeth. Chocolate was my favorite, but sometimes I had strawberry, like the day of the grossest thing that ever happened to me at St. Génevière's.

By then I was in second grade—*well established in the world of academia*, as my uncle the college professor would describe me. It was the first week of November, and I was well ahead of schedule in putting away my Halloween candy. All that sugar had turned my blood to caramel and my boogers to soft brown nougat. If you eat like a trash can, sooner or later you'll start to feel like one. That's what I learned through hands-on training one day in Sister Glenda's science class.

She was trying to teach us how there's water in the air, but we didn't believe her. She explained that everything is made of molecules. If you take something like a drop of water or a pizza and chop it up small enough, you'll get all the way down to molecules. And molecules are so small, they float around in the air and you can't even see them. When your grandma is baking cookies, you're actually smelling floating cookie molecules.

Now Sister Glenda didn't tell us this, but I think sometimes when you walk into the bathroom and you smell something spooky, you'd better keep breathing through your nose. You might not have considered it, but there are worse things than smelling poop. It seems to me that if you breathe through your mouth so you don't smell it, you might end up eating a bunch of floating poop molecules, and that can't be good for you. They'd probably reform in your esophagus, and then you'd have some explaining to do when the doctor looked at your x-ray.

Sister Glenda showed us how the windows were a lot colder than the air in the room. "That's why the window gets foggy!" she said, and she made a fist and pressed the side of her hand against the window. Then she tapped the window five times over the spot she'd made with her hand. When she stepped back from the window, there was a little baby footprint on the glass! "You see, sometimes water molecules bump into something cold, and they stick there and turn into drops big enough for you to see!"

Then she gave us worksheets about molecules. The first thing I always did whenever I got a worksheet was to sniff it. I wouldn't want to walk around smelling like purple worksheet ink, but I did like the smell—at least until that day. When I pressed the molecule worksheet against my nose, it smelled like a wet hound. In fact, I'd begun to notice everything smelled like a wet hound that morning, but the worksheet was especially gamy. All of a sudden my arms got cold and all the spit in my mouth dried up. I put the worksheet on my desk and stared at it. For a moment there were two of them. I looked up to see if Sister Glenda was nearby, but she was on the other side of the room talking to Clark about a bad word he'd just said to Nina. I didn't want to do my molecule worksheet anymore. In fact, I didn't like science anymore. My throat tickled like I'd swallowed a nest of tent caterpillars, and a couple of them were trying to climb up the back of my tongue.

I was going to throw up.

It was terrible. I'd never thrown up anywhere but at home, and my mom and dad had always been there. There are times when I get mad at my dad—usually after a spanking—but when I feel like I might throw up, he's the go-to guy. I want him there even more than Mom, because Dad holds my head up so it doesn't fall in the bucket. Throwing up is the loneliest thing in the world, because when you're done all you want is a hug, but everyone else just wants to step back and say *Eew*.

I thought about Martha, who had just tattled on Clark for calling Nina *stupid*. Back in first grade we took a field trip to the zoo. It took us an hour to get there, and we saw all the monkeys, some of the fish, and none of the birds. I didn't mind missing the birds. You don't need to go to the zoo to see a bunch of birds. When we got back on the bus to go home, Martha told Sister Dorothy Louise that she didn't feel well. Martha had eaten three sausage dogs and a bag of French fries, and then wished she hadn't. The bus had just gotten onto the highway when Martha upchucked in the aisle. It was the watery brown kind, and there were bits of French fry in it.

We didn't even get to say *Eew* before she threw up again. Then we all said *Eew* really loud to make up for missing our chance earlier. Sister Dorothy Louise—sometimes Sister Glenda called her Sister Dot Louise, but I don't think she liked it—and Sister Barbara turned around in their seats to see what was going on. Sister Glenda didn't have to turn around. She recognized the smell. Nothing smells like vomit. Not even dog vomit smells like vomit. Just the smell of vomit can make people vomit, and that's even before they see it. Jeff Spundt got to smell it, see it, and hear it, so then he vomited, too. It looked a lot like Martha's, but Jeff hadn't eaten French fries, so there were differences. But it all got down into the grooves in the aisle, and after we went up and down a couple hills, nobody could tell whose vomit was whose. We just lifted our feet and opened the windows until we got back to St. Géneviève's. Sister Dorothy Louise called Martha and Jeff up to the front of the bus and made them sit by themselves in the two front seats. For the next forty-five minutes they looked like the loneliest people in the world, and nobody wanted to give them a hug.

I didn't want to throw up in Sister Glenda's room: Jeff Spundt was just two seats down after all. I didn't want to go downstairs to the boys' room either, because I was worried I might have to lie down once I got there. There are cockroaches that won't lie down on that nasty floor. The girls' room was just around the corner from Sister Glenda's room, and for once I wasn't afraid of getting caught walking in there. I slid back my chair and stood up. The whole room tilted like a broken card table as I stumbled toward the chalkboard. I was halfway there before I realized I was still carrying my pencil. I turned and looked back at my desk, but it was a football field away, so I just let my pencil slip out of my hand. As I reached the chalkboard and began to write my name, my whole body tightened like I was a giant toothpaste tube that God was squeezing from the middle.

I've always liked those fancy ketchup packs they hand out at hamburger restaurants. I'm a mustard-lover myself, but I always get a bunch of ketchup packs because they're so much fun to play with. They sound like wet baby farts when you line them up on a hot sidewalk and ride over them on your bike. (Just don't do it anyplace where your mom will make you clean it up.) Once I tucked eleven of them under my dad's back tire, and ketchup sprayed all over the place, pretty much the same way my stomach contents sprayed all over Sister Glenda's chalkboard.

I looked over at Sister Glenda, who stared back at me like I had smashed one of Mama Hockenberry's prize watermelons against the wall. And it sort of looked like I had. That morning's breakfast-in-an-envelope fanned across the chalkboard like I'd done it on purpose. I hadn't gotten my hand out of the way in time, and barf was beginning to run down my arm inside my sleeve. A fair amount of the stuff had pooled on

103

the chalk ledge, and just before I heard the *Eew*, I heard a faint drip-drip-drip on the floor.

I thought Sister Glenda would be upset, but she was calm as she left Nina and Clark and started toward me. "Class," she said, pausing in the center of the room so everyone could hear, "if you feel that you are about to be ill, I would prefer you just make your way to the restroom without stopping to write your name on the chalkboard. We'll iron out the problems with the rules later." As if to add an *Amen* to what she had just said, I barfed on my shoes.

Sister Glenda took me by the shoulders—she wasn't my dad, but she did make me feel less alone—and guided me out of the classroom. We headed around the corner toward the girls' room, where I heaved once more in the doorway. I'd never been in the girls' room before. It was clean, and although it didn't smell like flowers, it didn't smell like the boys' room downstairs either. *Girls must have better aim*, I thought, as Sister Glenda led me to the nearest stall. I threw up once or twice more, and then I felt the firm, confident hands of Sister Glenda leading me by the shoulders to one of the sinks, where she wiped my chin and helped me wash my hands. Throughout my bout of sickness, I couldn't help being disappointed that there weren't any girls in there at the time.

Sister Glenda held the girls' room trashcan in front of me and helped me down the Grand Staircase and up the east wing to Sister Carrie in the nurse's clinic. Sister Carrie told me to lie down on a bed in the corner while she rooted around for a thermometer. The bed looked more like a short black couch without a back or arms, with a white paper sheet on a roller. The paper crackled like dry leaves when I lay down. I didn't think a bed like that would be very good for sleeping because the paper would wake you up every time you rolled over. As I lay there staring at the ceiling, trying not to bite the thermometer Sister Carrie had stuck under my tongue, I could hear Sister Glenda in the next room talking on the phone to my mom.

"Mrs. Larkin," I heard her say, "in my ministry I have been in the presence of countless sick people. And as a teacher I have seen more than my fair share of children regurgitate." I had never heard that word before, but I was pretty sure it meant *to puke all over a chalkboard*. "Now Mrs. Larkin, I have seen many a child vomit, but never *pink*." Her voice faded as I fell asleep on the couch-bed-thing, but I think she might have asked my mom what she had been feeding me.

One day, years from now when I am sixty, I might again meet Sister Glenda. I'll be bald, and so will she. We'll have to yell so we can hear each other. But even if she won't recognize my face or my name, I'll bet she'll remember the grossest—and the pinkest—thing that ever happened to me at St. Géneviève's.

Recess with Sister Glenda

Mr. Larkin! Did you place a toad in Miss Campbell's jacket hood?

Who, me? Are you kidding? Those things are sick! They have warts! They pee all over your hands! They have germs!

I didn't ask you if toads had germs, Mr. Larkin. I asked you if you placed one in Miss Campbell's jacket hood.

Yes, Sister Barbara. I did. I'm sorry.

****

It was, without question, one of the most amusing confrontations I had witnessed in fourteen years of teaching at St. Jenny's. Out on the lawn stood Nina Campbell, red-faced and ready to chew barbed wire; her friend Martha McRory standing by for moral support, yet trying not to laugh; and Sister Barbara, clutching a fat toad and towering over poor Timothy Larkin. I think even the elder sisters abed in the Convent knew he was guilty; it was a simple matter of getting him to admit it. As clever as that little guy was though, he was no sneak. Barbara could read him like she could the Beatitudes, and he knew not to lie. He just tried to evade the issue a bit. I had to give him points for clinging to a degree of integrity.

Barbara was an interesting woman—still is, most likely. She put up a tough exterior because she felt it was necessary for the students to understand proper conduct and respect for authority from the outset. I see her point, but I am just not wired that way. I try, but if a youngster pulls off a particularly clever caper, I find it difficult to maintain a straight face while meting out discipline. She dropped the facade though, when the kiddoes were not looking, and I could catch glimpses of the pony-tailed field hockey terror she used to be in college.

"What do you plan on doing with the toad, Barb?" I asked, after Timothy had been reprimanded and set on his way. Nina was not satisfied, but I doubt she ever could have been. I wonder what she would have done had it occurred to her that he was nearly as smitten with her as he was with the Dorazio girl. It was hardly common knowledge, but from my vantage point, it was obvious. The boys pick on the girls they like the most. I suppose the reason he never picked on Valerie Dorazio was that she was three inches taller and way out of his league. Nina was accessible, however, and thus bore the brunt of his shenanigans. And I wonder how Timothy would have reacted had he known the depth of affection Martha felt for him. Ah, the things you notice when the kids don't think you're looking!

Barbara cradled the toad in her hands, a Kleenex strategically placed beneath its leaky underparts. "I don't know, Glen," she chuckled. "Do you think Gwendolyn needs a toad?"

"She'd have us both defrocked and excommunicated," I giggled, taking the toad from her and thumbing in Timothy's direction, "unless she thought *he* did it!"

"Timothy Larkin," Barbara mused, shaking her head and gazing across the lawn to where Tim and Clark were darting in and out among the oaks. "Just look at him run!"

For fifteen minutes each day after lunch, Tim and Clark wore grooves into the sidewalks running through the oak grove. Usually they pretended to be fighter planes, their arms outstretched, spit flying as they fired imaginary machine guns. Their arms were outstretched today as well, but they had their hands in the pockets of their coats, which were held inside-out over their heads like fleshy membranes. I had just taught them about pterodactyls, so they were giving the fighter planes a rest.

"Evidently, pterodactyls look for nests of wool and polyester to drop their young," I said, stroking the toad and thinking about Nina's hood. I turned the toad in my hands so I could meet its blank stare. It gripped my fingers with its forelegs, its throat pulsing like a trip hammer. "I wonder what this little fellow is doing above ground. It's getting pretty chilly."

Barbara took the toad back and looked into its eyes. "Maybe there's more grasshopper to him than ant," she commented, alluding to Aesop's fable. "Precious few insects patrolling the grounds these days, I'm afraid."

I told her to guess what Timothy had done in class today, and she rolled her eyes and said she did not want to know. "Eight pages!" I said. "The rest of class finished . . . five, maybe?"

"That's the way he is," Barbara said, shaking her head again. "He pays attention with one eye and half his brain, and more often than not, he gets the right answer. But it's that *other* eye and the *other* half of his brain that you have to watch out for. I asked the class the other day why we double the final consonant in certain verbs before adding *-ing*. Do you know what he told me? He said, 'The same reason there's two M's in *Timmy*.'"

I was never very good with grammar—I always found it dull—but I told her I didn't think that was the correct answer. "No," she laughed. "But it shows you how the wheels are always turning. He's going to be a trial lawyer one day."

"Actor. Broadway," I argued. "A born ham."

She told me about the morning she proctored his St. Jenny's entrance exam. "I had six kids in there: the Campbell girl and the McRory girl, the Bernard boy, two boys who ended up at other schools, and Timothy Larkin. The test was orally administered, and the entire time he either scribbled on the margins of his answer booklet or pretended his pencil was some sort of helicopter. It drove me to distraction.

"Plain and simple, I was afraid to look at his responses. They were nearly impossible to decipher, but once I got a handle on his penmanship, I was amazed. One answer after another: correct, correct, correct. He outscored the lot of them!"

This time we both shook our heads. "What do you do when he's off his medication?" I asked.

"Ugh!" she shuddered. "I pray and duck—not always in that order!"

I smiled as she throttled her brass hand bell and gave it a shake, signaling the hopscotchers to stop hopping and the pterodactyls to come in for a landing. We guided the students back inside, where the humid air would mix with the redolence of their preadolescent perspiration—not yet the acrid quality that would accompany the fire of their hormones in the years to come.

****

Sister Carrie, may I see you for a moment, please?

Yes, Sister Gwendolyn?

Sister Carrie, did you see any children loitering about my office today?

No, the hall has been quiet all day, Sister Gwendolyn. Is everything all right?

No, Sister Carrie. It seems some prankster has placed a toad in my desk drawer.

Four Little Elves

B efore there was frost on the pumpkin, before the Thanksgiving turkey was basted, and even before I threw up pink all over Sister Glenda's chalkboard, Sister Helga began work on the 33rd Annual St. Géneviève's Christmas Operetta. Sister Helga—our music teacher whose ankles, you recall, overflowed her shoes like seventeen ounces of turkey milkshake in a sixteen ounce black leather mug—seemed resolute in her goal of running a tight ship. As a result, we approached the entire enterprise with trepidation, for Sister Helga was a creature to be feared. For one thing, operetta practice was held not in the Dungeon, but in the auditorium, with its parquet floor and high ceiling. How did she manage to climb all those stairs? And if she could climb stairs, what was to stop her from coming to our homes?

And if for some terrible reason she were to come to our homes on Halloween, would she be looking for candy, or something warm and wiggly and a whole lot chewier?

From the neck down, Sister Helga looked like she might really like candy. She could've hugged four kids at once, and that's normally a pretty good thing. From the neck down she had a genuine, open-armed, hey-kids-come-in-for-a-landing appearance to her. But from the neck up she resembled some sort of vicious hippopotamus-bat. She had a broad jaw that would have suited a rugged cowboy in one of those shoot-'em-up movies that people's uncles like to watch. As part of her greater face, though, it disappeared beneath her freckled pink cheekbones, which jutted out below the caves of her eye sockets like the parapets of a fleshy medieval castle. From the neck up, Sister Helga didn't look like she liked candy—at least not the type of candy that doesn't scream and bleed.

One summer day my dad took Charlie and me to the zoo so we could watch the four o'clock shark feeding. At three-fifty, the sharks were just moping along in big boring circles. They might have even been sleep-swimming. Their mouths ajar, gills fluttering like the sails of a catamaran riding a lazy surf, they looked very un-scary.

Then, at the stroke of four, the man with the Greatest Job In The World threw a salmon head the size of a Mitey-Mite football into the tank. The sharks woke up in a hurry, and they all looked pretty cross. From all corners of the tank shot a dozen yellowish-brown blurs with black eyes and angry teeth. The man threw in more fish heads and some other things I couldn't identify—probably broken pelicans—scattering the parts all over the surface of the water so the sharks wouldn't bite each other.

Nothing sank more than a foot or two before being swallowed whole. I thought it was great. Charlie, who will probably grow up to be a philosopher or something, went on and on about how "those poor salmons swam all the way upstream from the ocean, just to have their heads cut off and fed to sharks." I told him to relax, the heads were left over from when the bears ate breakfast, but I don't think it made him feel any better.

But that's just nature, isn't it? The baby salmon eats the minnow and grows up a little, goes for a dip in the ocean, eats a couple donuts, lays a few eggs in the shallow water where it was born, then it becomes lunch for a bear. The bear poops, a little beetle bellies up for a snack, goes for a swim (after waiting thirty minutes for its meal to settle) and then gets eaten by a salmon. *Voila*—food chain. So you see, there's a little bit of bear poop in all of us, but Sister Helga looked like she might eat it right out of the can.

At this point my mom would ask me to pause, please, and ponder deeply on what I just said. Sister Helga doesn't really eat bear poop. Nobody really eats bear poop. I don't even know what stores might sell bear poop, or even how it might be packaged.

But before we drop the issue of eating bear poop altogether, consider what we discovered about floating molecules in Sister Glenda's class. When you're hiking through the woods and you suddenly smell bear poop, remember to keep breathing through your nose, or you might end up eating bear poop after all. Of course, then it would be best to glance over both shoulders to make sure the bear isn't sneaking up on you. Don't waste time checking your shoes until you know the coast is clear. There are, indeed, worse things than eating or stepping in bear poop.

(In my defense, let the record show that Sister Helga only *looked* like she ate bear poop.)

During the first rehearsal, she herded Clark, Richard, David, and me into a little circle. The four of us thought we were goners. In my mind I raced through the entire catalog of misdeeds and indiscretions I had committed in her class, cross-referenced them against those involving any or all of the three boys standing with me, and then ruled out the two or three incidents I figured she didn't know about. It left nothing to my recollection that we could be in trouble for.

Then I reconsidered. Sister Helga clearly stood before us, miles from the Dungeon, probably by some nefarious and arcane means. I had read how vampires, for instance, can assume a gaseous state and float through cracks in walls and under doors. Thus it was safe to assume she knew everything I had ever done, plus two or three things I'd end up doing sometime down the road. I didn't believe she was a pure vampire, though. For one thing, she always wore a silver crucifix, and for another, if anyone at St. Géneviève's was a vampire, it was more likely Sister Gwendolyn.

"I want you four young men to be my elves," Sister Helga proclaimed, resting a beefy hand on David's shoulder and another on Clark's. I wasn't sure who had it worse: David and Clark for buckling under the weight of her paws, or Richard and I for standing more directly in the big woman's line of sight. Later we called it a draw.

Elves! Our little minds revved with the implications. We would make toys! And if we made them, surely we'd get to test them before loading them onto Santa's sleigh. *Santa's sleigh!* We'd get to ride on Santa's sleigh!

"I saw a play once in town," Richard said, "and this guy all dressed in green flew all over the stage." We listened spellbound: I'm sure all our mouths hung open. "Anyway, he didn't *really* fly," Richard continued. "Sometimes you could see the wire he was hanging from. But it was still really cool!" We knew exactly what Richard was talking about. I mean, *so what* if we weren't really going to be flying? How often do you get to dangle from a wire over a stage?

What Richard failed to explain, and what our moms read from the wardrobe list for elves, was that we would remain flat-footed on the floor decked in rubber pointed ears, felt slippers with little bells on them, and green hose. Not the kind of hose you use to wash your bike, but the kind you put on a girl. Our spirits fell faster than Peter Pan would if his trusty wire rusted and broke. It would still be a couple years before I'd get beaten up for the first time, but looking back on the entire green-hose-and-slipper debacle, the four of us figured it could happen to any one of us at any moment.

Green hose and slippers . . .

. . . *Man.*

In truth, I can't say what the operetta was about. There was so much going on in that cold auditorium, and Sister Helga's ship never seemed as tight as she would have liked. It took months of practice, with lots of yelling from Sister Helga (mostly at the elves) and the choir singing the same songs over and over. Kids' parents, like Mrs. Hockenberry and Mr. Diorio, helped out, and they sometimes yelled at each other.

"Stand here, kids, and when the soldiers march in, you'll have to—"

"They can't stand there because that's where we'll be putting the Christmas goose."

"We're talking about a prop the size of a card table. It's not the Christmas ostrich, after all. And I absolutely wish someone would instruct this little girl about the unsanitary implications of constantly sticking her fingers in her mouth!"

"That little girl happens to be my daughter."

"Well then, I guess that makes it all right . . ."

My fellow elves and I spent most of the time benched on the front row in the shadow of Sister Helga and her grand piano. It was a good ten degrees colder in her shade. At times though, we were required to wait backstage for our cues. Hearing Sister Helga remind us of our cues reminded me of Grandma Larkin, who always tells me to mind my Peas and Cues. I don't know what that means, but our operetta cues were easy. When the curtain opened for the second act, we were supposed to run onstage to sing our song:

> *Four little elves, such news we bring*
> *Rest now dear folks and hear us sing.*
> *In the Wintry Wild we'll set the scene*
> *For the crowning of the Winter Queen!*

The Winter Queen was played by a big sixth grade girl named Constance Kepple. Constance yelled at me and the other elves almost as much as Sister Helga did, and she told us several times to shut up. Telling someone to shut up isn't a very godly thing to do, and for all the times Sister Helga yelled at us, she never once told us to shut up. Constance also had allergies, so she blew her nose almost as much as she told people to shut up. The sound reminded me of Old Variable at the Hockenberrys' farm. I always thought a queen should be beautiful, sweet, and gentle. To me, the best queen in the world was Queen Sarah Saturday of the Neighborhood of Make Believe. She never told anyone to shut up, and if she ever blew her nose, she probably did it in the castle powder room with the door closed. Constance was less like a queen and more like an idling dump truck.

After we would sing our song, Sister Helga was usually too preoccupied with the next number, "The Promenade of the Polar Bears," to herd us back to our seats on the front row. That gave us the opportunity to explore the Mysteries of Backstage. There were thick ropes and curtains so heavy we could hardly lift them. Richard found a stack of cellophane squares in every color of the spectrum. Mr. Diorio told us later they were called *gels*, and that they were used to color the stage lights. That was fine, but we liked them because of how funny they looked when we wrapped them around our faces and made blowfish lips.

It was while we elves were exploring the backstage area that we realized we were directly beneath our homeroom. It didn't seem like anything could have been located above the stage because of the living blackness obscuring the high ceiling, as if a low sky of petroleum smoke loomed over the lights with their gels, the Wintry Wild, and even Dumpy Constance the Winter Queen herself. A set of black steel double doors at the rear corner of the backstage area opened into a plain cinderblock foyer unlike the rest of St. Géneviève's ancient construction of plaster and carved wood. I liked this foyer and its adjacent stairwell because they smelled like a freshly opened bag of caramels.

The moment we set foot into that rear foyer, a shared wordless impulse spurred us up the Caramel Staircase. Unlike the other staircases, this one was not decorated at all. The walls were painted the same color as my little pills—eggshell, my mom would call it. It was a tight staircase with only seven or eight steps between landings, and a long way up to a landing with any windows. When we reached the second floor, we pressed our noses to the glass and gazed across the lawn. We ran and played on that lawn every day, but we'd never seen it from quite that angle. But sure enough, we were on the far end of the north wing. Across the landing from the window stood a pair of French doors. We peered through their square window-panes down the yellowed hall of the north wing second floor. It was like we had always seen it, but from several steps back. It meant we were close to our homeroom, and probably within sniffing distance of Sister Barbara, who always seemed to have a guardian angel nearby, ready to point her eyes in my direction. I suddenly longed for the oddly safe and comforting chill of the shadow at the feet of Sister Helga and her grand piano. The staircase stretched upward into the gloom, but we would not achieve its heights that day. The summit of the Caramel Staircase would have to wait. And wait it did, until the second act of the Saturday night performance of the 33rd Annual St. Génevieve's Christmas Operetta, when the mighty elves of the Wintry Wild vanquished the wicked Hell-Mouse of the Treacherous Alpine Crags.

But that's someone else's story.

Prometheus Unbuttoned
(Musings from Sister Helga)

Just lately my feet hurt. I still have most of my joy, but it does not extend to my feet. And I must confess, it rarely appears on my face. When I was a girl I would run with my sisters from one end of our Bavarian village to the other, teasing the skinny boys with our pigtails and irritating the cattle drivers. But that was before my feet hurt so much. Mama was a seamstress, always sore and stooped, her fingers dotted with pinpricks, eyes lined from years of squinting and threading needles. It was uncommon in those days for mothers to be anything but housewives—a noble profession, but one that does not earn monetary compensation. She deemed it necessary to master a trade and supplement Papa's income, for Papa was but a lowly musician.

That is not to say he was a humble peasant. Papa was a man of great pride and musical skill, and he housed those qualities beneath a hearty veneer of blubber and jollity. He was certainly not a handsome man; indeed, one frown from him could send all the rats scrambling back into Hamlin. It was fortuitous then—at least for the so-fair citizens of Hamlin—that he seldom frowned. Instead he most commonly could be spotted stamping out some rollicking tune in one of the several beerhouses about the village, his massive, deceptively dexterous hands wringing sound from any of a slew of instruments he had mastered. I loved Mama, but found her company taxing on the days her head ached, so I found my solace in the company of my father among the raucous masses. It was during those times that I cultivated a taste for good beer, rich food, and passionate music.

119

Mind you, an overabundance of beer and sausage can be unhealthy, but music is nothing if not nurturing and healing. The music stirred me from the start, but I did not discover its subtle power and beauty until I heard Beethoven. While visiting family in Vienna I heard a performance of *Eroica*, his Third Symphony. The title simply means *Heroic*, and it was inspired by Beethoven's early impressions of Napoleon. At sixteen I went away to study the classical composers, to write, and to perform. I learned their histories, their successes and failures, and their idiosyncrasies. I would come to love Bach for his eye and ear—really, his heart—for the sacred, but I loved Beethoven for his fire.

That is precisely why I decided to teach. I discovered and embraced music of all forms, seeing it as a gift from Heaven. Just like Prometheus, that character from Greek mythology who took fire from Mt. Olympus and brought it to Earth, I found my mission in bringing the Gift of Music to the masses. Instead of performing it, as my father did, I chose to teach it, in hope that perhaps a handful of the thousands of children I have seen would go on to perform, as my father did.

Back when my feet were happy—or at least not so unhappy—my wanderlust drew me to the United States. There my interest in the musical mingled with an increasing interest in the spiritual. I befriended a young nun named Gwendolyn, who shared my love for music, though she would be hard pressed to carry a tune, even if it came fashioned with handles and a pushcart. She invited me to Sunday Mass, and although I initially found her off-key screeching of the sacred hymns distracting, I could not deny her love for their message. I came to appreciate her sincerity, then to admire it, and then to envy it. Soon enough I joined the Convent and embarked on my own path of spiritual devotion.

I fiddle-faddled about, teaching piano and guitar, and she taught history and religion for a time before becoming a fine principal. I have followed her ministry quite closely and have used it as a measuring stick for my own. The rest of my story twists and turns over the highways and hedges of wizening, widening, and aging. I would tell it to you now, but it has nothing to do with why my feet are sore.

Yes, music is nurturing and healing. But I am pragmatic, and I know that even the best medicines meet their match against age. A cancer patient will tell you that sometimes the cure is worse than the disease. I have not hiked in a long time. I lost my pigtails three-score years ago, and I grew up to look like my father. Just lately the task of teaching music—immersing myself into what has always been a tonic, but for the sake of assigning a grade to reluctant participants—has made me quite tired. When I inaugurated the Annual St. Géneviève's Christmas Operetta, it was a labor of love, with an emphasis on love over labor. Very little labor. But the rising costs of production, squabbling parents, and my waning abilities to keep pace with feisty elves one-tenth my age have wrought a sad transposition between labor and love.

As punishment for bringing fire from Heaven, Prometheus was bound for eternity to a rock as vultures picked at his innards. When the vultures had taken their fill, his innards were rejuvenated, only for the vultures to return to feed again. Lately it feels as if the squabbling parents and the feisty elves have been nibbling at my innards.

Yet moments of rejuvenation come, sometimes from the most unlikely places. The 33rd Annual St. Géneviève's Christmas Operetta provided one such moment. During the preparations for that performance, the vultures took their fill and then some, but then they brought a tiny morsel back.

I had assigned the elf parts to Masters Irwin, DeFloria, Larkin, and Bernard. Given their behavior as second graders, I figured they were not fit for any other role. Besides, should any one of them prove himself a promising musician, there might yet be a 34th Annual St. Géneviève's Christmas Operetta—or so I assumed at the time. Those four boys behaved as well as could be expected. Better, even. At times it seemed they were not in the auditorium at all.

121

There were parents bickering with each other over whose child made the prettiest snow pixie or the mightiest polar bear. I often wondered what was missing from their own childhoods that they deemed a priority in their children's. At one point the Christmas goose lay in Sister Natalie's art room in a state of disrepair—its paper maché innards had suffered greatly in their own right—and a playground ball was used in its stead. Each time it appeared in the dialogue, the word *goose* was replaced with *kickball*, to the great amusement of everyone under twelve.

Then came the evening of the performance. The goose lay restored and resplendent on the royal Christmas card table, the polar bears sparkled under the spotlights in their bleached pelts, and the Snow Queen's tiara was pinned fast in place. The elves hit their cues impeccably, and more importantly, they delivered their lyrics perfectly. Once they were safely offstage, I could relax and allow the performance to run itself. The Friday evening performance, vultures aside, was a success. Saturday's should succeed as well, I reasoned. I returned the next afternoon with as close to a spring in my step as I had in years.

That was before we knew about the rodent.

The props for the Annual St. Géneviève's Christmas Operetta were stored in an empty classroom on the third floor, two flights up from the stage. One of the polar bears had forgotten to remove his costume before enjoying a snow cone following the Friday performance, and he spilled a sizeable amount of cherry syrup down his chest. He looked as if he had just wandered in fresh from devouring a seal. No one had much hope for the stain to come clean; indeed, there was justifiable concern the costume might fall apart in the wash. At length Mrs. McRory hit upon the idea of spray painting over the stain.

It was a minor hurdle, I reassured myself. I had fetched up on America's shore with more lint in my purse than change, and I had carved my way out of that predicament. Certainly I could trust the problem of the bloodstained polar bear to re-solve itself.

Resolve itself, it did. But as is so true of modern life, one thing led to another. While applying paint in the upstairs prop room without sufficient ventilation, Mrs. McRory thought she saw a small black form scurrying along one of the base-boards. Of course, her panic spread to her daughter Martha, who had not seen the intruder, but soon believed she had. In-evitably the rat mania spread throughout the company, students and parents alike.

It should be noted that I am not fond of rodents. Yes, they are small, but that very quality allows them to appear and disappear at will. They climb, and they can jump. They have yellow teeth and ink-black eyes, and they are not to be trusted. Mrs. Hockenberry, who lived on a farm and was accustomed to dealing with many of God's creatures—both the lovely and the unlovely—did her utmost to assure us we had nothing to fear. Perhaps it was her confidence that enabled Masters Irwin, DeFloria, Larkin, and Bernard to do what they did.

Saturday evening's performance began much as Fri-day's had, with Sister Beryl's kindergarten class calling the assembly to order with the Recitation of the Christmas Letters. One of the polar bears would appear a little less *polar* than it had the previous evening, and Mrs. Hockenberry's words proved to be of little comfort to me as I groped with my feet in the darkness for the piano pedals. I am a woman of faith, and I believe my faith saw me across the world so many years ago. But in those moments as the house lights darkened and the cur-tain rose on Sister Beryl's students, I felt certain that at any moment the dastardly rodent would make his stage debut by prancing across the top of my shoe. Then there would be a spring in my step for sure.

During the intermission I attended to a minor adjust-ment in the Snow Queen's solo, for she suffered a touch of lar-yngitis and was laboring with the high notes. I also met with a pair of guests who had driven in from out-of-state to watch their granddaughter, who played the front portion of a caribou. It is understandable then, that when I heard that Masters Irwin, DeFloria, Larkin, and Bernard were not accounted for, I could expend but a limited amount of energy worrying about them.

They soon turned up.

The house lights dimmed for the second act, and as I began the piano fanfare to signal the raising of the curtain, which in turn signaled the elves to the stage, I could hear beyond my line of sight a hustle and bustle backstage inappropriate to the piece. A horrible clamor ensued: stage parents shouted, heavy objects lurched, and one small girl screamed. And onstage, nothing happened.

I rolled through the fanfare again, abandoning the restraint of my office and driving my weight into the keys as if I were Jerry Lee Lewis himself. Perhaps the elves had missed their cue due to the commotion backstage. No sooner had the thought crossed my mind than I dismissed it. I knew: the elves were the *cause* of the commotion backstage.

"Just get out there!" I heard one vexed parent bellow.

Suddenly, from a flurry of curtain erupted Masters Irwin, DeFloria, Larkin, and Bernard in their elf paraphernalia, but somehow altered as they performed their number. I struggled to keep my place on the musical score while simultaneously trying to discern what was wrong with the boys.

Their elf costumes were garish to begin with, so I did not instantly notice the Roman helmet Clark Bernard wore or the African spear Richard Irwin brandished. David De Floria wore a pair of red plastic shoulder pads and held a hammer. Timothy Larkin wielded the sword that complemented Clark Bernard's helmet, and at length I noticed a small bow and arrow set slung over his shoulder. They sang merrily, but moved through their jig with uncharacteristic swagger. The audience shared a puzzled pause before easing into a conservative round of applause for the boys as they finished their performance.

It was not until they turned to exit that I noticed Timothy Larkin's hand balled in a fist. He hesitated at the curtain and our eyes met. As his mates scurried past him and into the shadows, he held out his hand, revealing the plump corpse of a mouse.

"We got it, Sister!" he shouted, nearly out of breath. "We got the mouse! We got him for you, Sister! We all went up—" I missed what he said next because at that moment a well-muscled adult arm lashed out from the darkness, yanking Timothy Larkin from my sight.

Funny. My faith was sorely tested when I saw those four junior hooligans bouncing through the production in full battle regalia. When Timothy Larkin opened his hand and revealed their trophy (plucked from a trap Mr. Unger set, bless him), I hardly felt forgiving, but I felt desperately relieved.

So now I sit, finally able to muster a chuckle over the Great Mouse Crisis and the 33rd Annual St. Génevière's Christmas Operetta. I was Prometheus.

No, I *am* Prometheus. I feel a bit foggy as I sit here, the collar of my habit loosened now, a necessity for the past few years as I have continued to expand. I demand order in my classroom and reverence for the music. My prayer as a teacher is for my students to find the passion, the fire—in music, in faith, and in every corner and balcony and stage of life. I *am* Prometheus.

Sister Prometheus.

The Snow Angel

January was a lot of fun when I was in second grade. The snow was wonderful (or terrible, depending on who was talking). School was canceled four times that month, and Charlie and I made a snow fort. Charlie cried a lot during construction, especially when he got a bunch of snow down the back of his coat—stuff like that always happens to Charlie when we play together—but we did a pretty good job. Then I had Clark and Andrew over. Mom invited two of Charlie's friends also, and I was afraid they'd mess up everything, but they stayed inside and played with Charlie's Legos. Clark thought it would be a good idea to hide in the fort and throw snowballs at girls when they walked up the street, but we had one problem: the snow fort was in the back yard. We tried to pick up the fort and move it to the front, but it broke. So we went inside and played Legos with Charlie.

But like I said, not everybody liked the snow. One night, after he came home from work, my dad had to stay outside and shovel the driveway. It was icy, and before he was finished, I heard him say some new words I would have to ask Mom about. Shoveling snow is hard work. Even though it's very cold outside, you break a sweat in a hurry. I helped my dad one night, and it didn't take long before I thought my arms would fall off. The shovel just got heavier and heavier. That must have been what happened to Sister Dorothy Louise the night she tried to shovel the path around St. Génevève's.

We came back to school on a Friday after one of our unscheduled breaks. I thought it was a waste of time, since the weekend was just around the corner. When my mom dropped us off, Sister Gwendolyn was standing in the driveway in a wooly black parka, and instead of her veil, she wore a hat

127

shaped like a hairy beehive. She looked like a normal person. But something was odd about her appearance—maybe a bit more stooped. Mom seemed to think so too, so she parked the car and got out. She told us to run along, but when we got to the porch we turned around and watched them talk. Mom had her hand on her mouth, and before she started back to the car, she gave Sister Gwendolyn a hug. Sister Gwendolyn hugged her back. Something wasn't right. Charlie asked me what was wrong, and I told him to shut up and go to class.

Sister Barbara met me outside my homeroom and helped me off with my coat, which she had never done before. She smiled as she hung it on my peg out in the hall, which I thought was very sweet, but the way she told me to get seated and get busy made me think I was in trouble. Most of my classmates were already in their seats with their work in front of them, but they weren't really *doing* anything. I sat down in my desk next to Martha McRory and made fun of her haircut. Her mom always cut her hair, and sometimes you could tell. Nina told me I was *so* immature, and they both turned their seats toward the wall. Cheryl Diorio, who sat in front of me in homeroom, took her fingers out of mouth and told me I didn't have any manners.

I was used to that sort of treatment from Nina and Martha, but Cheryl rarely said a word to anyone unless she was talking about her rabbits. I looked all around me for something normal, but even Irwin and DeFloria were looking at me funny. *"What?!"* I demanded.

Herman Meier spoke up. "Something happened to Sister Dorothy Louise. She got sick in the snow."

I thought she might have thrown up. Maybe dealing with Martha and Jeff barfing on the bus finally caught up with her. All sorts of pictures popped up in my head about Sister Dorothy Louise jumping out of bed with her hand over her mouth, running down the hall, throwing open the front door, and throwing up in the snow. It sounded gross, but not the kind of thing that would make everyone in the building act so spooky.

"What do you mean, she got sick? And why didn't she just go to the bathroom?" I asked.

"She's dead, you moron!" Nina snapped. "Geez, Timothy, you're so stupid. You, too, Herman." She and Martha rolled their eyes. Herman looked at the floor, like he was sorry he had said anything. He was the only one who had, though, and I discovered I liked him better than I'd thought. There was really nothing wrong with him that a bath and a Kleenex couldn't fix.

I leaned his way and asked him what happened. There was no way Sister Dorothy Louise was dead. That kind of stuff just happened to old people—older people than Sister Dorothy Louise, anyway. In a quieter whisper than before, he told me she had fainted while shoveling snow. Then they had a tough time waking her up.

"*Who* had a tough time waking her up?" I asked. Herman shrugged. Everyone seemed sad, but no one wanted to talk about it. And anyone who did want to talk about it didn't know anything. It all seemed too important to forget about, as my dad sometimes tells me to do. I decided to ask Sister Barbara. She probably wouldn't want to talk about it either, but I didn't think she'd get ugly like Nina had. I got up from my seat and walked into the hall, where Sister Barbara was helping Clark with his coat, and I asked her what had happened to Sister Dorothy Louise.

Sister Barbara put a hand on my shoulder and one on Clark's, and she told us that Sister Dorothy Louise had been shoveling the snow off the sidewalk outside the Chapel the night before, and that she had collapsed. Somebody asked if she thought it was a heart attack, and she said probably so. "She was gone by the time the ambulance got here," Sister Barbara said. "I don't think she felt any pain at all."

At first I couldn't imagine any of it. "Was it like she fell asleep on her feet?" I asked. Clark added that his grandfather died of a heart attack, too.

"Sort of," Sister Barbara said. "Why don't you boys go into the room, now? I'll be along in just a minute." I could tell she was sad, but I thought it was nice that she talked to us about Sister Dorothy Louise. Then a weird thing happened when I sat down. I looked at the other kids in my class, and I didn't want to talk about Sister Dorothy Louise, either. I just wanted to think about her.

I hadn't known her very well, but everyone knew who she was. She looked serious, like Sister Barbara, but she laughed a lot. And she laughed big and loud, like someone had just told her the funniest joke in the world. She was almost as big as Sister Beryl and Sister Helga, but she moved a lot faster. You could feel the wind whenever she walked by. She always wore a grey habit that matched her eyes. She was pretty old—older than my grandparents, even—but she didn't wear glasses. That's how I know she had grey eyes. Once I got to see them close up when she was yelling at me for clomping down the hall like Frankenstein.

I thought about the Chapel and the sidewalk outside. I tried to picture Sister Dorothy Louise shoveling snow like my dad, but probably not saying all those words I had to ask my mom about. Maybe she just closed her eyes and went to sleep. She probably tipped over, and I wondered why that didn't wake her up. Maybe it did. Maybe she just lay there on her back like she was going to make a snow angel and stared up at the night sky until the doctor came. She could've gotten cold, though. I asked Herman if Sister Dorothy Louise was wearing a coat. He just shrugged. I'd have to find out.

We had all our normal classes that day, but the day wasn't normal. Sister Glenda had tears in her eyes in science. I'd never known anyone who'd died before, and I don't think I'd seen a grown-up cry more than once or twice. Grown-ups cry differently than kids do. First of all, they call it *weeping*.

They do it quietly, not like Charlie. When you grow up you don't cry when you hurt yourself, like bashing your head or cutting your finger. You just cry when something sad happens.

I asked her if Sister Dorothy Louise liked it when she called her Dot Louise. She laughed (Adults are weird; they can laugh and cry at the same time.) and said, "She didn't, but she did." Then she wiped her nose with a Kleenex. "Sister Dorothy has taught here at St. Jenny's for thirty-seven years. That's even longer than Sister Gwendolyn! She's like a mother to a lot of us, but she's more like my big sister."

All of a sudden it seemed like Sister Glenda was talking to the whole class, and not just me. "Once or twice a week we get together to eat pizza and watch TV. She loves baseball." *Wow!* I thought. *Nuns eating pizza!* Then I realized she was talking like Sister Dorothy Louise was still alive. I think she realized it too, because then she said, "She didn't think *Dot* sounded very dignified. We were such good friends though, that if I had ever called her Dorothy, she might have thought something was wrong."

Then she had to stop talking and get another Kleenex. She was weeping so hard she was almost crying. At home, when I cry or Charlie cries, Mom stops what she's doing and gives us a hug. Sometimes she still picks us up. None of us knew what to do with Sister Glenda. I wished her mom could have been there. It was the first time I'd ever considered that any of the sisters at St. Géneviève's had parents. They all seemed too strong and grown up to need any. I had learned a lot that day.

Sister Glenda threw herself into talking about how the moon pulls on the ocean, and the rest of class went by like things were fine. With everything I had figured out though, I knew things weren't fine. While everyone else was talking about ocean waves, I opened my tablet and made Sister Glenda a card. I drew a picture of a footprint on a window, then I put little molecule dots all around it. Inside I wrote *I'm sorry about Sister Dorothy Louise*, even though for once it wasn't my fault. I was too chicken to give it to her, but she picked it up when she saw me not paying attention. I thought she was going to be mad, but she smiled and told me how sweet I was. I was learning a lot, but I was also pretty confused.

I think the strangest part came after school, when I was heading out the front door with Charlie. Sister Gwendolyn was standing on the front porch, still wearing her parka. She was wearing her veil though, instead of the beehive, so I guessed she hadn't been standing outside all day. As I walked past her, trying not to look into her eyes, she put her hand on my shoulder and I froze. *What had I done? Did Sister Glenda tell her I was drawing in science?* "Young man?" she said, but it sounded nicer than when Sister Helga had said it the year before, like maybe I wasn't in trouble after all. "I want you to be extra good for you mother this weekend. She'll probably be very sad. She went to school here, you know. Sister Dorothy Louise was one of her favorite teachers." I stared at her, sort of surprised I wasn't turning to stone. "And she was one of my dearest friends." Her eyes were red, but not scary red. They were red like Sister Glenda's eyes had been. It occurred to me that when Mom picked us up, her eyes might look like that, too. Sister Gwendolyn put her arms around our shoulders and said, "Be good for your mother, now." Then she mussed Charlie's hair and told him to put his hat on.

Mom's eyes weren't red when she picked us up, but they were by the time we got home. I had too many questions for me to keep quiet, and before we pulled into our driveway, I had learned even more. I knew my mom had gone to St. Géneviève's, but I never considered that we knew some of the same people. She told me how Sister Dorothy Louise had taught her how to play Scrabble in the Lounge. She told me about her religion class with Sister Gwendolyn, and how Sister Gwendolyn had been so pretty back then, even under her veil, before arthritis twisted up her hands and shoulders. That led to more questions, which would have led to more if it hadn't started snowing again. Mom told me to go outside and help

Dad shovel the snow. She didn't have to tell me twice. I decided to look for Sister Gwendolyn Monday morning, just to say hi.

It all Started in the Convent

I finished my lunch quickly. There was work to be done. With the soggy wreckage of a PB&J still clinging to my teeth, I slammed shut my Dr. Doolittle lunchbox and scurried over to Sister Anna Rae, my writing teacher. I pestered her to the point of irritation—which was going some for Sister Anna Rae—until she gave in and told me today we would be learning lower-case x. She trusted me! She had leaned across her lunch table in strictest confidence and trusted me not to tell a soul!

I puffed out my chest and carried myself with a swagger for the rest of the afternoon, perplexing kids left and right with my knowing sneer. Sister Anna Rae had given me a map to the Treasure of Knowledge, and *X* marked the spot. Knowledge, a philosopher might say, illuminates Truth. And the Truth, as quoted in Scripture, will set you free. I was unaware of the liberating power of Truth at that point in my short career, so it comes as no surprise that I got the process backwards. Instead of Truth liberating *me*, I sought to liberate the Truth, which is what I accomplished in the early moments of that afternoon's writing class. "Today, boys and girls," Sister Anna Rae began, "we will learn to write the lowercase—"

"X!" I exclaimed, shattering my teacher's trust and startling Cheryl Diorio, who had been busy making sure she still had ten fingers. There'd been no reason for Cheryl not to have ten fingers—she'd had ten fingers the last time she'd checked them during lunch—she simply wanted to make sure. Sister Anna Rae gaped at me, as did the rest of the class. I knew I had crossed a line. It would be a long time before I would again be deemed worthy of bearing the Truth.

Nevertheless, Sister Anna Rae taught us the complexities of lowercase x— "a rolling hill and dale with a spear thrust through the bank for good measure," she said, sort of the way a flagpole might look after a cataclysmic earthquake. She demonstrated proper x-writing technique with great sweeping gestures of her black-sleeved arm, which rose and swooped in the atmosphere like a hyperactive crow who'd forgotten to take his pill.

We assumed our stations at the blackboard and began drawing—Sister Anna Rae always instructed us to *draw*—our letters. I began working my new letter into words: boxes, fox, mix. Clark stood two stations to my left, and soon we were challenging each other with erasers. It's funny how an eraser loaded with chalk dust looks like a minor explosion when smacked against an object—especially a classmate's back.

"Is all that dirt coming from you or the eraser?" Clark coughed amid a cloud of dust after bopping me a good one. I didn't answer in words, but with violence, clocking him across the forehead with my eraser. Sister Anna Rae had just begun to intervene, a crimson glow of anger pulsating within the air around her, when we all heard the great iron bell tolling in the Gold Staircase beyond the kindergarten room.

A fire drill! I'd been wondering when we would have a fire drill. I had been in only one before, but it had been terribly exciting. We filed into the hall, snaked down the Grand Staircase, and marched out the front door into the late-winter mist. We were all too thrilled to be bothered by the cold, and when Brian, a knowledgeable third grader, told us the fire alarm was somehow connected to the fire department, we all craned our necks to see the approaching fire engines.

But soon the cold set in under a sinking sky, and the vulture-claw treetops snagged the clouds. My disappointment grew as I realized the frayed cotton rope that rang the old iron bell couldn't conduct an electronic signal to the fire department. I knew that much. There would be no flashing lights and no sirens.

It hadn't occurred to me, however, that in an *actual* emergency, Sister Gwendolyn could simply pick up the phone and contact the authorities.

Sister Anna Rae stared at the building, almost as if she was looking through it, and I heard her say, "It's in the Convent." At first I didn't know what that meant, but it didn't sound like a very big deal. Probably a space heater had stunk up a classroom. Dust on the heating coils. I strolled over to a neighboring class to give them the good news—*Don't worry, it's just the Convent*—but I was reprimanded for my efforts and told to get back in line. It had been *months* since I had visited the Convent; how was I supposed to remember what the Convent was? At any rate, pushing Sister Anna Rae to anger was considered to be difficult in most circles, but I had already succeeded twice. And a lengthy afternoon still lay before us.

The mist turned to rain and I began to wonder if there wasn't something to the iron bell's ringing after all. I didn't remember the last fire drill taking so long. Why wouldn't they let us back in? Soon we were ushered to the faculty parking lot to wait in cars—actual *teachers'* cars! Sister Anna Rae decided that Clark and I should not be placed in the same automobile. For once I didn't mind, because moments after I was tucked into the snug confines of a strange Oldsmobile with seven classmates, a spectacular solar flare belched through the roof of the east wing. At once I forgot my partner in crime.

We sat in silence and watched the flames absorb the roof. Shingles rippled in the heat and disappeared into the burning abyss of the attic as entire sections of decking caved in. Soon there was nothing left of the steep roof but fire, and the grey clouds above were replaced by pulsing dragon wings of smoke. The windows on the third floor, with their fancy pointed arches, shattered in the heat and fire roared out of them. *We learned French in one of those rooms.* I thought about the French nametag I had made for myself on an index card, and I wondered what would happen to *le Petit Prince.*

137

A string of fire trucks pulled into the circle drive beyond the east wing. Some pulled onto the lawn while the rest continued around to the back of the school, toward the Convent and Chapel. Through it all, I hadn't considered the people inside until a parade of elderly nuns filed through the front doors, rolling in wheelchairs pushed by the younger sisters and nurses. One of the old sisters was wearing my heavy blue pea coat—so *that* was safe, anyway—but I still worried about Charlie and my Dr. Doolittle lunchbox.

We sat in the car and gawked at the fire as it worked its way along the third floor between the Gold and Green Staircases the way a rattlesnake works its way along a prairie dog. It never occurred to us that we were living every school kid's fantasy: indeed, our eyes *had* seen the Glory of the Burning of the School! You think you can imagine it because everyone has seen fire on TV. I'd seen the fire wolf down the forest in *Bambi*, and there's always something burning on the news at night. Kids all over the world wish for it, but seeing it was different. Our school was familiar, and we watched it die from the inside out.

It was like the neighborhood bonfire we'd built with our Christmas trees a couple months earlier. I'd gotten used to seeing that magnificent tree dominating our living room, and it made me sad to see how small it looked among all the other neighborhood trees when the fire rose up and squashed them all down. The next day Charlie and I walked back to the site to see if we could find our tree, but there was nothing left but ash.

The fire at school was worse than that. My dad once showed me that famous black-and-white picture of the *Hindenberg* blowing up. I think what makes that old picture so spooky is the way the zeppelin is half-hanging in the air. Fire is just beginning to run up the sides of the ship, and even though you know the whole thing is going to crash to the ground in just a few seconds, everything's frozen in the picture. The nose is still strong and sharp, like nothing could be wrong. All we could do was to stare at our school as the flames worked their way from one familiar object to—*through*—another.

Before long, the car windows began to fog, and we smeared them with our hands to improve our view. None of us thought to recreate Sister Glenda's baby footprint on the glass. We knew we were witnessing a solemn event, even if we couldn't grasp the future implications.

Herman Meier, who likes fires, decided this was a bad fire, one he didn't want to watch anymore. One of the boys in my car mentioned that he'd seen Sister Ricarda guiding Charlie's class across the lawn while we were piling into cars, so I was pretty sure he was safe. A police officer in a long yellow raincoat directed parents through the teacher parking lot to pick up their kids, and when my mom pulled in, I jumped out of the car and ran to her. I didn't wait for Sister Anna Rae or Sister Barbara to come with an umbrella. When I was buckling in, I saw Charlie walking toward us from another direction, slowly, as Sister Ricarda shielded him from the rain with a small blue umbrella.

Rain blew into the car as Charlie fumbled with his door. Now I could smell the smoke and hear the fire. It sounded like something was chewing on the roof. Charlie got situated and buckled, and as Mom wheeled the car through the parking lot and out onto the main driveway, the flames and their prey gradually retreated into the oaks and the waning afternoon. We pulled out onto the highway and I watched over my shoulder as the smoke spread like a bruise in the sky over the trees. I thought about something Herman told me once about how things burn up and turn to smoke. They might blow far away, but they never *go* away. Looking back, I wasn't so sure.

Nobody said a word as dusk showed up early for its afternoon appointment, overcoming all but the blast furnace glow of St. Génevière's.

St. Florian's: the Little Red Schoolhouse
(Mom's two cents)

I kept expecting the boys to say something in the car, but they didn't speak. Knowing how Timmy, like Nature, abhors a vacuum, I kept quiet in hopes that he would sound off. But the sight of St. Jenny's in flames overwhelmed him. I must say, having attended St. Jenny's as a girl, I too had plenty to process. I would have stared at the holocaust myself, probably with my mouth agape like so many of the children, but my protective instinct drove me to get the kids out of there.

St. Jenny's burned on a Wednesday, and the kids enjoyed another unexpected vacation while Sister Gwendolyn and her staff reorganized. The kids played hard through the mornings and afternoons, mostly indoors to avoid winter's rainy surrender to spring. Charlie seemed to take the event in stride, as if, at some point after Christmas but shortly before Easter, it was tradition that school should burst into flames. I'm certain he believed the place would be up and running again the following week. Timmy, on the other hand, had begun to absorb the deeper implications by Tuesday. In the evenings he would become serious and ask if we thought the beeswax candle in the Chapel had melted. He persisted in worrying about the animals in their glass cases. Always on about the animals. By Thursday he realized he and his classmates couldn't expect to stay home from school for the rest of their lives.

In the end the building was lost. Only the exterior walls, small portions of the roof, and most of the first floor remained—essentially a burned-out shell. All of the students, faculty, and elderly sisters made it to safety, and only a handful of firemen suffered injuries. And those were minor.

The building has haunted me in my dreams. Two or three times a year I find myself barreling lawlessly through the halls of the Convent or bounding down the Grand Staircase, clearing three steps at a time. (I'll tell you on the sly, Timothy Larkin was not the only jester in St. Jenny's court.) Other times I fetch up in the basement corridor among the animals. They remain frozen in my dreams as they were in reality—as they remain to this day if they somehow managed to survive the fire.

But wherever my dreams of St. Jenny's begin, they invariably end in the Gothic Chapel, with its high vaulted ceiling and stained glass windows. I find myself walking not up the aisle, but on a catwalk mysteriously suspended far above. As I gaze upon the stone floor and the pews below, I never experience the uneasiness of height that I might in waking. Instead, if I remember my dreams correctly, I awaken with a sense of accomplished adventures.

Not surprisingly, there often follows a pang of loss. The building was more than just a school—a place where knuckles were rapped with a ruler following any of a thousand transgressions frowned upon by a veiled faculty. It was where I learned to multiply by nine and divide six-digit numbers. It was where I spent my days shivering in November, sweating in May. I never saw it as a sanctuary, but it was, now that I look back at those years so long ago, a source of *Right*. I recognize the stern tones of my teachers in my own voice when I need to correct my boys. And I think it's noteworthy that those tones give me comfort as I muddle my way through the dimly lit pathways of adulthood. I don't always see that path of Right, but the sisters at St. Géneviève's taught me that it's always there, someplace.

Sister Gwendolyn, her staff, and several priests of the local diocese toiled over the next two weeks to establish what some called St. Jenny's Junior—a temporary haven in the form of a small, red-roofed building at the Seminary of St. Florian on the other side of town. I thought the move was appropriate and ironic, as St. Florian is often depicted as a knight pouring water on a burning chapel. There the student body returned to school on a split session, with the secondary grades attending from six a.m. until noon and the primaries meeting from noon until six p.m.

The squat, beige-bricked building had a central hall connecting eight classrooms and a small office suite. There were no golden staircases, no sunken libraries, and no Gothic arches. There was nothing about the place, in fact, worth revisiting across the stream of dreams. How sad it would be for the kids.

(Sister Barbara Wraps Things Up)

That is true. St. Florian's did not offer the same—I hesitate to say *magical*—charm that we enjoyed at St. Geneviève's. Something special existed within the very walls of the old school. Sure, the same faculty carried on at St. Florian's, and we brought with us the same students, the same rules, and most of the books. But any good teacher will tell you that the complexion of the student body changes from year to year. There's a revolving door at the front of each school. Students graduate, students move, some students even die.

Many of us taught at St. Geneviève's from our twenties to our sixties, but a good many sisters were as fleeting and ephemeral as the students themselves. Even those of us who poured our whole lives into the place were fleeting if you choose to look at it a certain way. It's useless to consider your outward appearance.

This is what I look like.

No. That is what you look like *today*. You did not look quite that way a year ago, even if you wore your hair similarly. We would recognize you, but you were different. We might recognize you twenty years from now, but don't count on it. My dear friend and colleague Sister Glenda would tell you that your body is hard at work, constantly sloughing old cells and generating new ones. I am literally not the same person I was seven years ago, and you will not be the person you are seven years from now, let alone twenty. It reminds me of the old joke about the man who claimed to own George Washington's axe. Although the handle had been changed a couple times and there was a shiny new axe head, it was the same tool our nation's father used to chop down the fabled cherry tree. Sure.

But St. Génevieve's hardly changed. It breathed in and out with each passing class, and somehow rejuvenated itself just enough to remain standing. The oaks shading the front yard were already well established by the time I came along as a novice instructor. Years later when I returned to walk the weeded lot where the building once stood, they did not appear much different. The animals that glared with unblinking glass eyes at Timothy Larkin as he hid from Sister Helga's fury were the same ones that glared at me as I first toured the school with Sister Gwendolyn twenty years previously.

But the old school's passing marked a Changing of Things. Obviously, meeting on a split session at St. Florian's was impractical. And when the township fire marshal condemned the old building, the implications were clear. We felt as though there had been a death in the family. Reactions were bittersweet. The rooms at St. Génevieve's were cold in the winter, stifling in the spring and early fall. If I remained in my classroom long enough after the dismissal bell, I could expect small furry visitors, inspecting me with their beady eyes, wondering who I was and when I might be leaving their domain. The staircases had been taxed by several decades' worth of thundering loafers and oxfords, and they had begun to tax my poor knees in return. St. Génevieve's turned out to be the gruff uncle who would often argue for the love of stirring up trouble, but also the one who would be just as quick to pass along a humorous anecdote or an unexpected bear hug.

The building burned on the Ides of March. We polished off the last three months of the academic year at St. Florian's Seminary (or as Glenda called it, St. Flo's Refugee

Camp for the Poor Huddled Masses). Summer came and the sisters of our order scattered across the United States like dandelion seeds. And as we followed the winds of God's direction, the body of St. Géneviève's lay in state among the vivid green of the oaks standing as stoic pallbearers. Leaves fell in autumn, and with them fell shingles from the sagging roof. By the time winter came, the skeletal rafters complemented the bare trees surrounding them.

Life returned to the trees the following spring, but the halls of St. Géneviève's remained quiet as a tomb. Vandals broke out windows, and intrepid teenagers on summer break dared each other to roam the unlit catacombs of the basement. The building fell to the wrecking ball that September, eighteen months after the fire dealt its decisive blow. Great bulldozers pushed imported earth into the yawning chasm where young explorers used to dare.

I returned to the grounds a few years later for Sister Gwendolyn's Burial Mass up on the hill. After the ceremony I walked through the gap in the trees that opened onto what used to be the back lawn. I was not prepared for the sprawling expanse of grass that greeted me, but as I approached the great oak grove on the far edge, I found my bearings. I stood in silence where Sister Gwendolyn's office once stood, and I looked skyward over the neon leaves of spring.

I prayed for my colleagues, and I prayed for former students who would one day become my colleagues. I prayed for the Timothy Larkins who pass through this life, sometimes learning from their skinned knees, many times not. If they never manage to shake off their impulsive bent, if they plead to God in vain for its removal as did St. Paul over the thorn in his flesh, perhaps they should see it as a gift that, once mastered, might elevate them to heights their parents could never imagine. I wish I could see them all. Dandelion seeds, students, and teachers—leaves that darken through summer, turn golden, and then fall in autumn.

Like the sacred halls of St. Géneviève's.

About the author

Robert M. Kissner

Robert M. Kissner grew up in a suburb of Pittsburgh, Pennsylvania, where he developed a love for reading, writing, music, sports, and exploring the woods. He earned his Bachelor's Degree in Christianity and Psychology at Houston Baptist University, and his Master's Degree in Literature at the University of Houston-Clear Lake. His thesis title was *Pressing the Nose to the Glass: Themes of Transformation in the Poetry of Randall Jarrell.*

He served as a youth minister in the Houston area for eleven years before turning his attention to teaching. He has taught in the San Jacinto College District and the Houston Independent School District, and currently he teaches Language Arts at McCullough Junior High School in the Conroe Independent School District.

In addition to his work in the classroom, he has received dozens of accolades and awards for public speaking through Toastmasters International, and he is a percussionist for the Conroe Symphony Orchestra.

Made in the USA
Lexington, KY
21 December 2014